# Roadcraft

## the Police Driver's Handbook

D0262558

The Stationery Office
London

Authors: Philip Coyne, Penny Mares, Barbara MacDonald

Design, photography and illustration:
Bill Mayblin – Information Design Workshop

Research: Philip Coyne, Bill Mayblin, Penny Mares

Project management: Dr Barrie Irving, Police Foundation

Background research in Human Factors and Psychology:
Dr Lisa Dorn and Dr Julie Gandolfi, Driving Research Group,
Department of Human Factors, Cranfield University

The Police Foundation wishes to thank Dr Gordon Sharp and
the Scottish Police College for kind permission to adapt
material from *The Human Aspects of Police Driving* in
Chapter 1.

## The Police Foundation

The Police Foundation is a wholly independent charity
dedicated to using high quality evidence to improve policing
for the benefit of the public.

For further details of the Foundation's work and publications
contact:

The Police Foundation
First Floor
Park Place
12 Lawn Lane
London SW8 1UD
Tel: 020 7582 3744
Fax: 020 7587 0671

sue.roberts@police-foundation.org.uk

Charity Registration Number: 278257

Applications for reproduction should be made in writing to
The Stationery Office Limited, St Crispins, Duke Street,
Norwich NR3 1PD

New edition 2007

ISBN 978 0 11 702168 6

Printed in the United Kingdom for The Stationery Office
on 75% recycled material

N5484787 10/07 C100

# Acknowledgments

This new edition of *Roadcraft* was initiated by the Police Foundation at the request of the Association of Chief Police Officers and other users of the text. It was produced in consultation with members of the National Police Driving Schools Conference.

The Police Foundation would like to thank them and the many other individuals and organisations, especially the Institute of Advanced Motorists, who gave so freely of their time and expertise in the preparation of this edition of *Roadcraft*.

This edition of *Roadcraft* has been approved by the Association of Chief Police Officers, which is satisfied that it reflects current best practice in police driver instruction and takes into account the relevant views of civilian experts.

Other essential guides to safe driving also published by The Stationery Office include:

*Motorcycle Roadcraft – the police rider's handbook to better motorcycling*
ISBN 978 0 11 341143 6

*Towing Roadcraft – the essential towing handbook*
ISBN 978 0 11 552022 8

To order or find out more about these or any other driving titles, please refer to the contact details printed inside the back cover of this book.

# Foreword

*Roadcraft* is the official police drivers' handbook.
This edition, like its predecessors, has been prepared
after careful consultation with senior police driving
instructors and others with experience in advanced
driver training. It incorporates the best and most
reliable parts of the older editions with the latest
knowledge in this rapidly developing field. While
designed to be complemented by expert instruction,
*Roadcraft* is a valuable text for all drivers who wish to
raise their skills to a higher level.

On behalf of the UK Police Service

# Contents

Chapter 3

## The system of car control

# About *Roadcraft*

## How can *Roadcraft* help you become a better driver?

*Roadcraft* is the handbook for police drivers undertaking police driver training. In police training *Roadcraft* is combined with practical instruction. This edition is designed so that it can be used for self study either before or during a course, and for ready reference afterwards.

The aim of *Roadcraft* is to improve your driving ability. Your safety and that of other road users depends on your awareness of what is happening around you and your ability to control the position and speed of your vehicle relative to everything else on the road. A collision or even a near miss is often the result of a lapse in driving skill. *Roadcraft* aims to help you become a better driver by increasing your awareness of all the factors that affect your driving – your own capabilities, the characteristics of your vehicle, and the road and traffic conditions.

The *Roadcraft* system of car control is a methodical approach to hazards which increases your safety by giving you more time to react in complex situations.

## What vehicles does *Roadcraft* cover?

You can apply the principles of *Roadcraft* no matter what vehicle you drive. It is written with a modern car in mind but is also relevant to older and larger vehicles.

The basic design and the supplementary features built into a vehicle all affect its capabilities. With the increasing sophistication in vehicle design and safety technology, it is not possible in a book of this size to cover the range of variations in wheel-drive, transmission, adaptive suspension, active safety feature, etc. Know your vehicle's characteristics and adapt your driving to them, and have an understanding of the manufacturer's guidance for every vehicle that you drive.

## What *Roadcraft* does not include

*Roadcraft* assumes that you are thoroughly familiar with the current edition of the *Highway Code* and the *Know your Traffic Signs* booklet.

Special techniques such as those used in emergency response or pursuit driving and other techniques that require a high level of instruction to ensure their safety are not included. Your instructor will introduce you to these when appropriate.

## Using *Roadcraft* for self study

The main learning points of each chapter are listed at the start under 'Use this chapter to find out...'. This list will help you choose the chapters or sections that you need to concentrate on.

Illustrations and diagrams are used to explain complex ideas. Read them along with the text as they often expand on this or provide a different level of information.

Important points are highlighted in light blue boxes.

The questions and activities in the text are designed to help you check your understanding and assess your progress. Many of the activities are practical, helping you to transfer the advice in *Roadcraft* to your everyday driving.

The review of the key points and questions at the end of each chapter are to help you check your understanding. You may find that writing out answers to the questions helps you learn.

## Working through the chapters

Chapters 1, 2 and 3 set out the basic principles and information on which later chapters build so you should ideally read these in sequence first. If you are using *Roadcraft* as part of a driving course, your instructor may suggest you study certain sections of the book in a different order.

## The importance of practice

Just reading *Roadcraft* will not make you a better driver. Practice is an essential part of learning any skill. What matters is not how well you can recall what's in this book but how well you can apply what you have learnt to your driving. Many of the techniques explained here are fairly simple in themselves. Finesse in driving ability comes from applying them consistently. All the techniques depend on judgement and this only comes with practice. Aim to apply the techniques in *Roadcraft* systematically so that they become an everyday part of your driving.

You cannot absorb all the information in *Roadcraft* in one reading, so we suggest that you read a section, select a technique, practise it, assess your progress, and then refer back to *Roadcraft* to refine the technique further.

## Using *Roadcraft* for reference

Cross-references throughout point you to relevant information in other chapters. The contents pages at the front of the book list all the main headings and a selective list of the most useful sub-headings. There is an index on page 173 and a glossary of key terms on page 169.

## Learning is a continual process

Being a good driver means that you never stop learning. *Roadcraft* offers advice on the principles of better driving but cannot be a definitive guide to all driving situations and techniques. Vehicles and driving conditions are constantly changing, and your skills need to keep pace with this change, otherwise they could become outdated, inappropriate and dangerous. Aim to constantly review and, where necessary, adapt your driving so that you maintain high standards and continually improve your techniques. Whenever you drive, use it as an opportunity to assess and further develop your *Roadcraft* skills.

# Chapter 1
# Mental skills for better driving

**Use this chapter to find out:**

- the mental skills that can help you become a better driver
- how your brain processes information and how this affects your driving
- the effects of operational driving stress on driving performance
- how to recognise and counter unhelpful attitudes and emotions
- physiological factors that can affect your driving ability
- how to assess a safe speed
- how self assessment can improve your driving and safety
- why knowing your vehicle is vital for safe driving.

This chapter looks at the mental skills and attitudes that are essential for police driving. These will enable you to make the most of the driving skills that you will develop through training.

*Roadcraft* begins with the psychological aspects of driving because this is what determines how you use your vehicle, and how you respond to road conditions and to other road users. A central aim of *Roadcraft* and police training is to help you develop the mental skills and attitudes that will enable you to deal with complex driving tasks calmly and safely at all times.

The first part of Chapter 1 summarises some of the key concepts in the companion handbook used in police training, *Human Aspects of Police Driving* by Dr Gordon Sharp. The psychology of driving is an expanding area of research and, across the European Union, driver training at all levels places increasing emphasis on mental skills and attitudes.

See European Goals for Driver Education, page 167, for further information.

The final part of Chapter 1 discusses the important related topic of speed and safety.

# Skills for police driving

As a police driver, your working life is characterised by the number and variety of different tasks that you must carry out, often within a single shift. A day that starts with a routine patrol might end up at the scene of a multi-vehicle collision on the motorway or in a fast pursuit. Whatever the driving task, you are expected to maintain the highest possible standard of driving and to complete the job in hand calmly and efficiently. All drivers need to develop both technical and mental skills, but there are certain elements that are particularly important for the operational police driver. These are:

- **multi-tasking** – being able to carry out several complex driving tasks at the same time and with equal accuracy and efficiency

- **alertness** – being vigilant and remaining focused so as to spot potential hazards early and leave nothing to chance

- **attention distribution** – splitting your attention across all aspects of a driving task

- **situational awareness** – using all your senses to build up an accurate mental picture of the operational environment

- **anticipation** – using your observational skills and driving experience to spot actual and potential hazards and predict how the situation is likely to unfold

- **planning** – planning precisely and making rapid and accurate decisions throughout the task

- **making judgements** – judging situations accurately and taking safe and appropriate action.

See Chapter 2, *Observation and anticipation*, for a full discussion of alertness, anticipation and planning.

> ***Situational awareness is essential for police drivers***
>
> *This involves gathering, interpreting and using any relevant information to make sense of what is going on around you and what is likely to happen next, so that you can make intelligent decisions and stay in control.*

To achieve the highest standards of driving, you need to build up your existing skills, add to them the manoeuvres and procedures that are required in police operations, and expand the higher mental skills that you need for accuracy and safety. Developing these multiple and complex skills begins with training but is a process of continual improvement. It needs constant practice and accurate self assessment throughout your professional driving career.

Mental skills for better driving

# Developing your higher mental skills

To develop your driving to police operational standards, you will need to expand your higher mental processing abilities – and understand the factors that might impair your ability to process complex information. The diagram below shows how your brain processes

information. It explains the mental activities that enable you to choose the most appropriate action, check it for safety, monitor and if necessary adjust the action as you carry out:

- observation
- perception
- decision-making
- making a judgement
- action monitoring.

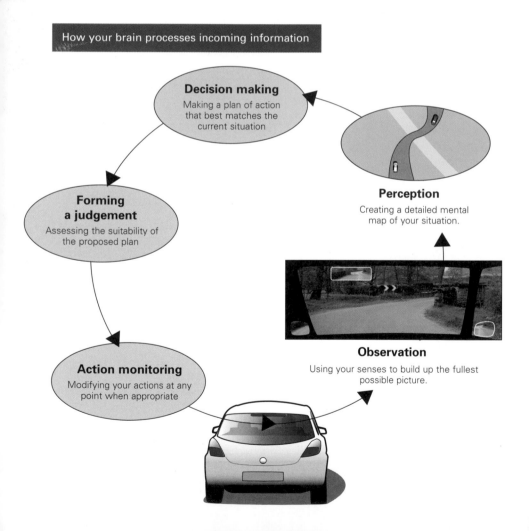

## How your brain processes incoming information

**Decision making**
Making a plan of action that best matches the current situation

**Perception**
Creating a detailed mental map of your situation.

**Forming a judgement**
Assessing the suitability of the proposed plan

**Observation**
Using your senses to build up the fullest possible picture.

**Action monitoring**
Modifying your actions at any point when appropriate

Safe driving depends on forming an accurate picture of the present situation and drawing on your previous experience to plan your next action safely:

- **Observation** – Vision is the most important sense for driving but you should learn to use all your senses to build up the fullest possible picture of yourself, your surroundings and your situation (see Chapter 2).

- **Perception** – Your brain uses your observations – and information from your previous knowledge and experience that is stored in your long term memory – to build up a detailed mental map or 'picture' of your situation.

- **Decision-making** – Your brain compares this model with situations from your previous experience, identifies what actions were taken in the past and selects or adapts a plan of action that best matches the current situation.

- **Forming a judgement** – Your brain assesses the suitability of the proposed plan by comparing it with actions that you have carried out safely in similar circumstances before. You use several types of judgement:

  - assessing the proposed plan for risk, noting hazards and grading them based on previous experience

  - anticipating how events are likely to unfold

  - assessing your space, position, speed and gear.

- **Action monitoring** – As you put your plan into action, your brain takes in new information and continuously checks it for accuracy, appropriateness and safety so that you can quickly modify your actions at any time. Developing this ability to a high standard takes experience and practice. You also need alertness and intense concentration to drive efficiently and safely in a rapidly changing situation.

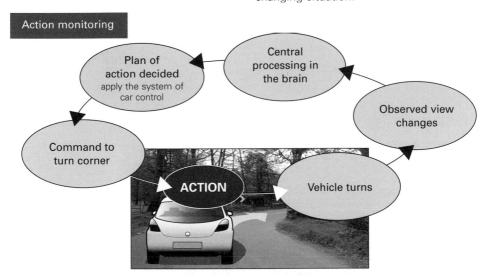

Action monitoring

Plan of action decided
apply the system of car control

Central processing in the brain

Observed view changes

Command to turn corner

ACTION

Vehicle turns

*The ability to judge a situation, grade risks and anticipate how things are likely to unfold is essential to safe driving, especially at high speeds.*

# Factors that affect higher mental skills

There are three important factors that can affect the mental skills you need for driving:

- **limitations on your brain's ability to process information**

- **operational driving stress**

- **your attitude, emotions and personality.**

# Your brain's ability to process information

The highly demanding nature of police driving means that the brain's information-processing capacity can become overstretched, reducing driving performance and compromising safety. If you understand the in-built limitations to brain processing, you can take steps to improve your information processing ability. The four key limitations are:

- reaction time

- errors of perception

- attention span

- memory storage.

## Reaction time

Your *reaction time* is the time between gathering new information about a hazard and responding to it.

**Reaction time = decision time + response time**

**Decision time** is the time between observing the hazard and deciding what to do.

**Response time** is the time to start the physical response.

Most drivers have a similar response time **but they vary greatly in the amount of time they need to decide what to do.**

As situations become more complicated, you need more decision time and so your overall reaction time will also be longer. As a police driver you may be dealing with situations requiring many complex decisions and judgements – often under pressure and at high speed – where a delayed reaction can have catastrophic results. Using the system of car control (Chapter 3) gives you a structured method for rapid decision-making. Using a systematic approach reduces decision time and so gives you more overall time to react in complex situations.

## Errors of perception

In demanding situations like high speed driving, it is possible for a driver to observe the environment but fail to *perceive* information accurately. Common errors in perception are:

- **Illusions** – Certain things can deceive the eye; for example, untrained drivers often perceive a bend as being less sharp than it actually is so that they negotiate it too quickly and risk a skid or collision. *Roadcraft* and training will sharpen your observation and your ability to read the road accurately.

- **Habit and expectancy** – When you drive regularly on familiar roads, you get used to the route. Habit can prevent you from spotting a hazard

that is out of the ordinary – such as a vehicle emerging from a disused garage forecourt. Be aware that this mismatch between what you expect and the actual situation is a source of potential danger for professional drivers who regularly drive the same route.

- **Regression effects** – Drivers who switch vehicles regularly can, under pressure during a demanding operation, confuse the control positions with those of a more familiar vehicle, or try to drive a manual vehicle as if it were automatic. Taking time to do a thorough pre-driving check helps you 'rehearse' the controls and handling characteristics of the vehicle and can reduce the likelihood of confusing these with previously learnt routines.

## Attention span

Police drivers have to process information from several different sources through different senses at the same time – road conditions, radio traffic, navigation, the mobile data terminal, the nature of the operation, and so on. This affects driving performance because processing complex information can affect your perception and slow your reaction times. At times passengers, radio or other distractions may divert attention from important information, or add to the complexity of information that needs to processed. Through training and practice you can learn to select information, filter out the distractions and concentrate on the most important priorities. Giving a commentary can help you focus your attention during a demanding drive.

## Memory storage capacity

The brain can't always deal with all the information it is given. Memory is divided into three areas – working memory, short term memory and long term memory.

### Working memory

filters information entering the brain, sending it to short term memory or discarding it to make way for new information. In a complex situation this may happen before the 'old' information has been processed.

### Short term memory

holds limited amounts of information for a short time, after which the data is either transferred into long term memory or forgotten.

### Long term memory

can store large amounts of information for a long time – but information can be difficult to recall from your long term memory unless it is recent, used often or prompted by something in the present.

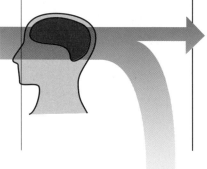

F O R G O T T E N

## Using your brain to maximum capacity

There are some things you can do to overcome these limitations and increase your ability to process information:

- regularly practise driving techniques and manoeuvres so that you can do them accurately and efficiently

- sharpen your observation and perception and develop your situational awareness

- use the system of car control whenever you drive so that you make decisions methodically and quickly (Chapter 3)

- learn to hold on to important pieces of information until you need them by repeating them, relating them to things you know well, or using other memory techniques that you find helpful.

# Driving stress

All professional drivers are vulnerable to driving stress, especially police drivers who regularly deal with difficult and hazardous situations. During a demanding or difficult drive where brain processing is already stretched to the limit, operational stressors can overload the system and impair decision and judgement making. Training aims to increase your mental processing and problem solving capacity, giving you more time to think and complete the driving task efficiently, which helps reduce the effects of driving stress.

Individuals respond differently to stressful situations so what you find stressful may not be stressful for a colleague, and vice versa.

*Be aware of your personal stressors (things **you** find stressful) during driving operations. Learn to recognise the emotional and physical symptoms of stress so that you can deal with them before they start to affect your driving performance.*

## Operational stressors

Police drivers are exposed to several types of operational stress:

- the anticipatory stress of facing a difficult or demanding task (e.g. anxiety about what you will find on arrival at an incident)

- the 'adrenaline rush' arising from a

sudden event such as an emergency call-out; a degree of arousal enhances performance but beyond this optimum level alertness and concentration tend to fall away

- stress related to aspects of the task – difficult traffic or weather conditions, navigation problems, lack of advance detail about an incident, time pressure

- the stress of being in a situation in which you or others may be exposed to extreme hazards

- stress arising from repeated exposure to distressing incidents in the past; aspects of a current situation may 'prompt' recall of distressing memories and the effect may impair current decision-making and judgement

- preoccupation with a previous error of judgement

- stress associated with work factors other than operational driving such as career problems or difficult working relationships which carry over into driving.

Research shows that repeated exposure to stress can make drivers more accident-prone and, in more severe cases, susceptible to stress-related illness. *Human Aspects of Police Driving* looks in more detail at the physical symptoms of stress and at other types of stress that can affect police officers.

# Practical steps to combat stress

- Use the techniques you learn in training and practise them continually – well-learned techniques are less likely to break down under stressful conditions. This is an advantage of using the system of car control (Chapter 3).

- Take care of your general health – get regular exercise and learn to relax.

- Develop a calm confident approach to your driving – keep in mind that you have the training and skills to deal with the situations you encounter.

- Where possible, share decision-making and work as part of a team.

- Stress can be cumulative so try to keep any domestic or social problems separate from work issues. Put other problems aside when you get into your vehicle.

- Don't dwell on previous stressful experiences or earlier errors of judgement.

# Attitudes and driving behaviour

'Attitude' is the state of mind with which you approach the driving task. An important goal of training is to help you develop a positive state of mind and avoid unwanted attitudes and behaviour. But under demanding conditions, even the most experienced police driver can sometimes experience negative attitudes through stress or tiredness. Under pressure, the individual may not realise this is happening or that it is affecting information processing and the ability to make decisions and judgements.

Personality tends to influence our attitude to life in general and so your personality has some effect on your attitude to driving. Other factors that have nothing directly to do with the driving task – domestic or financial problems, issues at work – can also affect your attitude and emotions while driving. Developing self awareness – knowing your personality traits and the things that trigger negative attitudes or feelings – can help you recognise and control unhelpful attitudes so that you can guard against them during demanding driving situations.

*Safe driving must be your primary goal at all times.*

Mental skills for better driving

## Stress-induced negative attitudes

Negative attitudes and behaviour patterns that police drivers learn to control or avoid through training have been observed to re-emerge under pressure in difficult and demanding conditions such as rapid response or pursuit. Some common reactions that you should recognise and avoid are:

- **impatience** – through a desire to get to the incident quickly
- **intolerance** – a belief that the importance of the task automatically gives the police driver priority over other road users
- **impulsiveness** – rushing decisions because time is short.

## Emotions caused by tiredness

During a difficult drive, police drivers often experience an initial high arousal state which later gives way to an 'exhaustive phase' in which tiredness sets in and alertness declines. Tiredness can also cause the release of powerful emotions that your training has taught you to suppress. Common emotions are:

- **anger or frustration** – for example, at failing to achieve the objective of the pursuit or at the pursued driver
- **personalisation** – getting into personal conflict with the pursued driver or person at the incident at the end of the drive
- **resignation** – avoiding making further decisions or avoiding taking responsibility for the outcome after a prolonged pursuit with no result.

There is more about dealing with tiredness in Chapter 2, *Observation and anticipation*.

# How attitudes and emotions impair brain processing

A demanding or stressful drive stretches your brain's capacity to process information. Stress and the release of negative attitudes and emotions can further affect your brain processing capacity in several ways:

- impairing your working memory so that planning, decision-making and judgement become slower and less accurate
- narrowing your visual field and reducing ability to scan so that your ability to read the road accurately is reduced
- limiting your ability to split your attention and assess hazards, making it more likely that you will take risks.

## Red mist

'Red mist' is a term that has been used to describe the state of mind of drivers who are so determined to achieve some objective – catching the vehicle in front, getting to an incident in the shortest possible time – that they are no longer capable of realistically assessing driving risks. Their minds are not on their driving but on some other goal; they have become emotionally and physiologically caught up in the incident. Another term sometimes used is 'target fixation'.

The key to preventing red mist is to concentrate on the driving task in hand rather than on the incident. You will need to develop your own strategy for achieving this, but there are some key steps you can take:

- **Don't get into a personality conflict with the driver you are pursuing.** Be dispassionate and concentrate on behaviour rather than personality; use neutral, non-aggressive language to describe the other driver (to yourself and others).

- **Don't try and imagine what you will find at the incident** – assess the situation when you get there.

- **Concentrate on driving** – giving yourself a running commentary can help you to focus on processing information and keep negative emotions under control.

# Other physiological factors

Some other factors can affect driver attitudes, emotions and behaviour:

- **minor illness** (colds, viral infections, hay fever, postviral states)
- **medication** (especially those causing drowsiness)
- **residual blood alcohol**
- **low blood sugar** arising from hunger
- **cyclical mood swings** caused by hormone changes (this applies to men as well as women).

Be aware of the things that can affect your driving behaviour and take steps to counter their possible effect.

## Practical steps to counter unwanted attitudes and behaviour

- Maintain a calm and professional approach to your driving, especially in emergency situations.

- Concentrate on applying the techniques you have learned during your training and use the system of car control (Chapter 3).

- Maintain a wide range of attention scanning and avoiding 'coning' of attention (red mist).

- Focus on the driving task in hand rather than what might be happening at the scene.

- Avoid 'personalising' other drivers, in thought or speech.

- Try to identify your own personality type and get to know the behaviour patterns it produces – especially the unwanted ones.

- Be aware of what is happening within your body and be alert to anything (hay fever, alcohol from the previous evening, hunger) that might affect your driving.

- Consider the consequences of making a mistake.

- Develop your self assessment skills (see below).

# Speed and safety

Speed has a major impact on safety and a central aim of *Roadcraft* is to equip you with the attitude and practical abilities to use speed safely.

One of the most important messages in *Human Aspects of Police Driving* – summarised in the section above – is that you need to know your own limitations to be a safe driver. The ability to use speed safely depends on:

- understanding how speed affects your perception and judgement

- always staying within the limits of your competence.

Drivers who drive fast regardless of the circumstances have a collision risk three to five times greater than drivers who don't. Your safety and that of other road users depends on your being able to accurately assess what is a safe speed. This depends on your driving capability, your vehicle's capabilities and the road and weather conditions.

## Underestimating speed

We looked at some common errors of perception earlier in this chapter. It is easy to underestimate the speed at which you are driving This is because your perception of speed depends on several factors:

- the difference in detail perceived by your forward and side vision

- engine, road and wind noise

- the evenness of the ride

- your idea of 'normal' speed

- the road – its width and whether it is enclosed or open

- your height off the ground.

Roadcraft

Below are some common situations where speed perception can be distorted:

- When you come off a motorway or other fast road onto a road where speeds below 30 or 40 mph are appropriate, you will feel as if you are travelling much more slowly than you really are. Allow time for normal speed perception to return.

- Low visibility – in fog, sleet, heavy rain and at night – can distort your perception of speed so you find yourself driving faster than you realise.

- If you drive a vehicle that is smoother, quieter or more powerful than your usual vehicle, you may go faster than you realise because you use road noise, engine noise and vibration, as well as sight and balance, to assess your speed.

- On wide open roads, speeds will seem slower than on small confined roads.

Always keep a check on your speedometer. Take particular care when you leave a motorway or fast road, especially at roundabouts.

## Using speed safely

At higher speeds you have to process more information in less time, so you must always allow for any other factors which may reduce your ability to do this, such as divided attention, stress, negative attitudes or emotions, or extreme tiredness.

*Always drive within your competence, at a speed which is appropriate to the circumstances.*

Whatever your speed, if it is inappropriate to the circumstances it is dangerous.

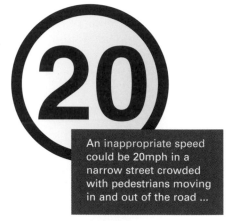

An inappropriate speed could be 20mph in a narrow street crowded with pedestrians moving in and out of the road ...

... or 60mph on a straight open road if you are tired and your attention is split between several tasks.

In this chapter we have looked at a number of internal and external pressures on police drivers that will at times encourage you to drive faster than your competence or the circumstances justify. Learn to recognise these pressures and take steps to counter them. Every driver has their own speed limit – this is the highest speed at which they are safe and comfortable in a given situation. Know your limit and never go beyond it.

The principle that you should always drive at an appropriate speed for the circumstances is central to the system of car control (Chapter 3) and you will meet the idea again throughout *Roadcraft*. It is most clearly expressed in the safe stopping rule:

*Always drive so that you can stop safely within the distance you can see to be clear.*

### Check your safety at speed

Over a journey of at least an hour, monitor your speed and whether you would always be able to stop within the distance you can see to be clear.

Assess yourself carefully – do you always keep to the safe stopping distance rule at higher speeds?

Mental skills for better driving

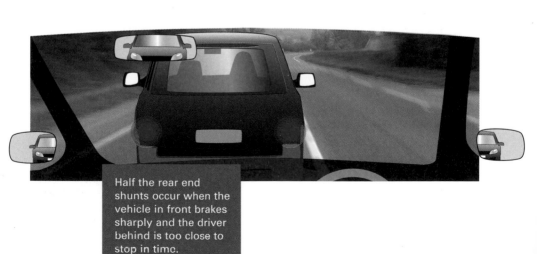

Half the rear end shunts occur when the vehicle in front brakes sharply and the driver behind is too close to stop in time.

# Accurate self assessment improves driving skills

Accurately assessing your own performance is central to developing your driving ability, both during and after training. As well as monitoring your actions as they are actually happening, you need to be able to review your performance after a drive. Being honest with yourself about what you did well and not so well is vital if you want to continue to improve. This means looking back on a drive to consider your situational awareness, your ability to anticipate and plan for hazards, and whether your attitude or emotions affected your performance, as well as considering your practical skills in using the system of car control and manoeuvring your vehicle. The first thing to focus on when you review a drive should be your own and other road users' safety.

Reviewing things that went well and analysing why you handled them well is also important. It will help you to transfer your actions in that particular situation to other situations, broadening your ability to make accurate decisions and judgements from the specific to the general.

Studies show that people who develop a high level of skill in a particular area have better than average self assessment skills. They are continually reviewing their performance, analysing their mistakes, and working out how they can improve. People who are not very good at assessing themselves find it difficult to develop a higher level of skill.

# Knowing your vehicle is part of knowing your limitations

A vital part of knowing your own limitations as a driver is knowing the vehicle you are driving and what it can and cannot do. During a demanding drive you cannot process information accurately and make safe decisions unless you are thoroughly familiar with the condition of your vehicle (e.g. tyre tread depth, brakes), its capabilities (e.g. type of fuel, type of drive), and how to use the controls correctly (e.g. type of transmission, type of active safety device).

*Always check your vehicle before you drive. See 'Know your vehicle' on page 164 for roadworthiness and pre-driving checks and brake tests.*

# Becoming a better driver with *Roadcraft*

*Roadcraft* will develop your awareness of traffic situations, and show you how to improve your observation and anticipation so that you can spot hazards early. It will explain how to use the system of car control to process information and make decisions and judgements efficiently and accurately, giving you more time to react in demanding situations and to negotiate hazards safely and smoothly.

Each chapter includes self assessment questions to help you check your understanding of police driving techniques and develop your driving ability to its full potential.

# Review

**In this chapter we have looked at:**

- why you need to develop your higher mental skills as well as your technical and operational skills
- ways to help your brain process information from your observations to maximum capacity
- how to recognise operational driving stress and steps to prevent it affecting your driving performance
- how attitudes and emotions can affect your driving performance and ways of countering negative states of mind
- being aware of your body and how physiological factors can affect your driving
- how to recognise and resist internal and external pressures that might compromise safety
- how this impacts on your speed
- how accurate self assessment can help you develop your driving skills and awareness of safety
- why knowing your vehicle is vital for safe decision making.

## Check your understanding

Why are higher mental skills especially important for drivers in the emergency services?

What are three factors that can impair the mental skills you need for driving?

What is situational awareness?

What is reaction time and how can you reduce it?

Give some examples of driving stressors that can affect your driving ability.

Describe some steps you might take to counter the effects of operational driving stress.

Give some examples of negative attitudes that can arise from driving stress.

Describe practical steps to avoid the effect of negative attitudes and emotions in police driving.

List four physiological factors that might reduce your driving performance.

What is the guiding rule to decide a safe speed?

Give two examples of pressures that might encourage you to drive too fast and how you can counter these.

Why is it important to know your vehicle?

If you have difficulty in answering any of these questions, look back over the relevant part of this chapter to refresh your memory.

# Chapter 2
# Observation and anticipation

**Use this chapter to find out about:**

- why good anticipation is vital to better driving
- how careful observation contributes to anticipation
- how to use your observations to make a driving plan
- how to improve your observation and anticipation
- how to adapt your driving to speed, night conditions, weather and road surface
- how to make the best use of road signs and markings.

# Why observation and anticipation are essential for better driving

This chapter looks at the skills of observation and anticipation, and how you can apply them to your driving. The first part of the chapter looks at the link between observation, anticipation and planning, and at how you can learn to observe more effectively. The second part looks at physiological factors that affect observation and anticipation. The final part looks at weather conditions and other important sources of information in the traffic environment.

An important goal of police driver training is to develop sophisticated anticipation skills. Anticipation is the ability to identify hazards at the earliest possible opportunity.

A **hazard** is anything which is an actual or potential danger. It's useful to think in terms of three types of hazard:

- physical features (e.g. junctions, bends, road surface)
- the position or movement of other people (e.g. drivers, cyclists, pedestrians)
- weather conditions (e.g. icy road, poor visibility).

A hazard can be immediate and obvious, such as a car approaching you on the wrong side of the road. Or it might be something less obvious but just as dangerous – for example, a blind bend could conceal an obstacle in your path. Failing to recognise hazardous situations is a major cause of collisions.

Observation is a key component of anticipation. Careful observation allows you to spot hazards and give yourself extra time to think, anticipate and react. You can then deal with unfolding hazards before they develop into dangerous situations.

Most of your observations while driving will be visual (around 95%) but you should also make use of your other senses such as hearing (horn sounds, children), smell (e.g. new-mown grass, possibly indicating the presence of slow-moving grass-cutting machinery) and physical sensations such as vibration (e.g. juddering from road surface irregularities).

But good anticipation involves more than just good observation. It means 'reading the road' and extracting the fullest meaning from your observations. This involves:

- using your higher mental skills to interpret clues in the environment
- developing your ability to scan your surroundings.

## Using your higher mental skills

You may occasionally have caught yourself driving on 'autopilot' – perhaps thinking about the incident you are driving to – and only noticing what is happening immediately in front of you. The ability to **take, use** and **give** information and to apply the system of car control (Chapter 3) requires concentration and your active attention to your driving all the time. Negotiating traffic situations safely means observing, reading the road, anticipating hazards and planning ahead.

Chapter 1 explained how you can expand your capacity to process information and develop your situational awareness. Use these mental skills to accurately interpret visual clues about the traffic situation and the likely behaviour of other road users.

# Planning

Safer driving depends on systematically using the information you gather from observation to plan your driving actions:

- anticipate hazards
- prioritise
- decide what to do.

Generally things do not just happen, they take a while to develop – good planning depends on early observation and early anticipation of risk.

The purpose of the plan is to put you in the correct position, at the correct speed, with the correct gear engaged at the correct time to negotiate hazards safely and efficiently. As soon as conditions change, a new driving plan is required; so effective planning is a continual process of forming and re-forming plans.

The diagram on the right shows how the key stages of planning encourage you to interpret and act on your observations.

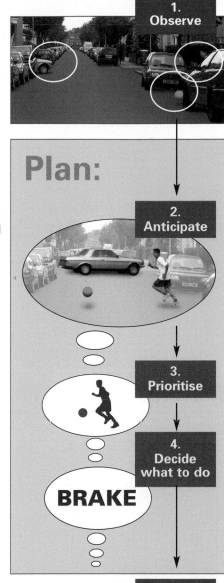

## Anticipate hazards

Research has shown that a driver's ability to anticipate hazards can be developed through specific training in hazard perception. But you can also learn to anticipate through experience, if you assess your own performance and that of other road users each time you drive. Young, inexperienced drivers typically react very quickly to simple hazards but tend to react more slowly to complex traffic hazards because they lack experience of the kinds of hazardous events that can lead to a collision. In other words, they are not aware of the risks and fail to anticipate them. Trained drivers spot the early signs of possible trouble and anticipate what might happen, so they react quickly and appropriately. They are constantly alert to potential danger and monitor risk at a subconscious level so that they are ready to respond quickly if the situation develops.

Observation and anticipation reinforce each other. On a familiar route, for example, you may know from experience where there are likely to be hazards, even if your view of the road is blocked by vehicles. Anticipating hazards sharpens your observation as you search the road for visual clues. From careful observation you gather new visual clues that increase your ability to anticipate.

You can develop your skill at anticipating the actions of other drivers by carefully observing their progress and behaviour, and their head, hand and eye movements. Even careful drivers can make mistakes, so learning to anticipate other road users' intentions can give you and them an extra safety margin.

*Anticipating hazards gives you extra time. The more time that you have to react to a hazard, the more likely that you can deal with it safely.*

**On your next journey, give yourself a running commentary as you drive:** describe what hazards you can observe and how you plan to deal with them. Remember to observe other drivers as well as their vehicles.

With practice you should find that you observe more hazards, earlier and in more detail, and gain more time to react.

## Prioritise hazards

## Decide what to do

Where there are multiple hazards, deal with them in order of importance. The level of danger associated with particular hazards varies with:

- the hazard itself
- how close it is to you
- road layout
- whether the hazard is stationary or moving
- how fast you are approaching it.

The greater the danger, the higher the priority, but be ready to re-adjust your priorities as the situation develops.

**Planning is a vital skill when you are driving.** Practise applying the three stages of planning during every journey until you do it automatically, even when you are driving under pressure.

The purpose of your plan is to decide on and adopt a course of action that ensures the safety of yourself and other road users at all times, taking account of:

- what can be seen
- what cannot be seen
- what might reasonably be expected to happen
- which hazards represent the greatest threat
- what to do if things turn out differently from expected (contingency plans).

If you plan your driving you should be able to make decisions in a methodical way at any moment and without hesitation.

While you are driving you should be continuously anticipating, prioritising hazards and deciding what to do. At first you might find it difficult to consciously work through these three stages all the time, but with practice this will become second nature and prove a quick and reliable guide to action.

# Improving your observation

Observation and anticipation depend both on visual skills – how you use your eyes to observe the environment – and on mental skills such as concentration and information processing. These vital skills are interlinked.

## Scanning the environment

Our ability to handle information about the environment is limited so we tend to cope with this by concentrating on one part of it at a time. But drivers who rapidly scan the whole environment looking for different kinds of hazards have a much lower risk of accident than drivers who concentrate on one area.

Imagine your field of view as a picture – you can see the whole picture but you can only concentrate on one part of it at a time. This is why you need to develop the habit of scanning repeatedly and regularly.

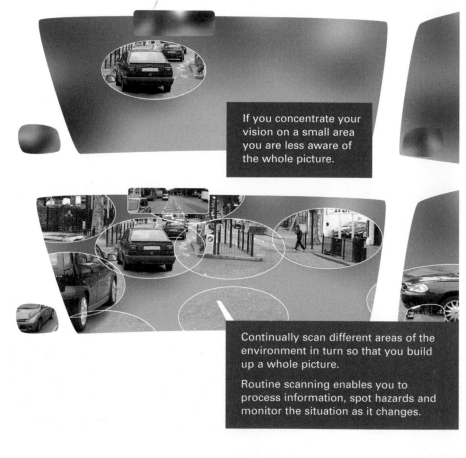

If you concentrate your vision on a small area you are less aware of the whole picture.

Continually scan different areas of the environment in turn so that you build up a whole picture.

Routine scanning enables you to process information, spot hazards and monitor the situation as it changes.

Learn to use your eyes in a scanning motion which sweeps the whole environment – the far distance, the middle distance, the foreground, the sides and rear – to build up a picture of what is happening all around you, as far as you can see, in every direction.

Scanning is a continuous process. When a new view opens out in front of you, quickly scan the new scene. By scanning the whole of the environment you will know where the areas of risk are. Check and re-check these risk areas in your visual sweeps. Avoid fixing on particular risk areas because this stops you placing them in the broader context. Use all your mirrors, and consider a shoulder check on the occasions when it is not safe to rely on your mirrors alone – for example, when reversing, moving off from the kerb, joining a motorway or leaving a roundabout.

## Looking but not seeing

What we see depends to a large extent on what we expect to see. At some time, you might have pulled out having missed seeing a bicycle coming from the direction in which you have just looked. Mistakes of this type are common because drivers are generally looking for cars or lorries but not other road users such as bicycles or motorcycles. When we concentrate we don't just look at a particular part of a scene, we look for particular types of objects in that scene. We find it easier to detect objects that we expect to see, and react more quickly to them. So we often fail to see objects that we don't expect to see.

Many people relax their concentration when driving along familiar routes, so it is important to give as much attention to observation and anticipation on routes you use every day as on journeys you are making for the first time.

When you scan, look out for solo road users.

If you are not expecting them they can become 'invisible' to you.

## Peripheral vision

Peripheral vision is the area of eyesight surrounding the central area of sharply defined vision. It gives you your sense of speed and your position on the road, registers the movement of other road users and acts as a cue for central vision. Learn to react to your peripheral vision as well as your central vision. The eye's receptors in this area are different from the central receptors, and are particularly good at sensing movement. This warns you of areas that you need to examine more closely.

## How speed affects observation

Adjust your speed to how well you can see, the complexity of the situation and the distance it will take you to stop. At 70 mph you would typically need to allow a safe stopping distance of about 100 metres. This is the distance between motorway marker posts.

See Chapter 4, *Acceleration, using gears, braking and steering*, page 73, The safe stopping distance rule.

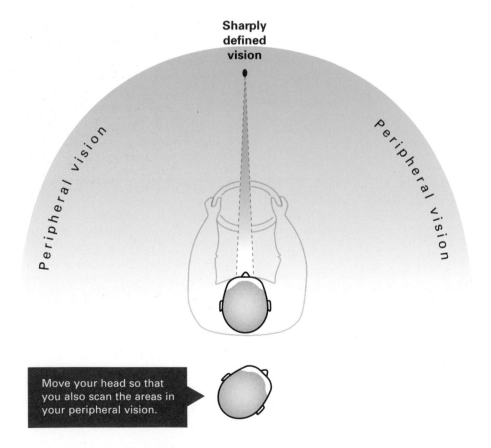

**Sharply defined vision**

Peripheral vision

Peripheral vision

Move your head so that you also scan the areas in your peripheral vision.

Remember the safe stopping distance rule:

**Always drive so you can stop safely within the distance you can see to be clear.**

is not the same thing as a safe speed. The safe speed for a particular stretch of road depends on the conditions at the time. It is your responsibility to select a speed appropriate for the conditions so that you maximise your ability to observe and anticipate hazards.

- The faster you go, the further ahead you need to look. This is because as you drive faster, the nearest point at which you can accurately focus moves away from you. Foreground detail becomes blurred and observation becomes more difficult because you have to process more information in less time. The only way to cope with this is to scan further ahead, beyond the point where your eyes naturally come to rest, to give yourself more time to assess, plan and react.

- Driving at high speed requires a high level of attention and judgement which you can't sustain if you are tired. Plan regular rest periods to help you to stay alert and get some fresh air. Rest for longer when tired.

- At higher speeds, you will travel further before you can react to what you have seen and you need to build this into your safe stopping distance.

- Your ability to take in foreground detail decreases with speed and increases as you slow down. In areas of high traffic density such as town centres, you must slow down so that you are able to take in as much foreground information as possible.

- Statutory speed limits set the maximum permissible speed, but this

The statutory maximum speed limit is not the same thing as the **safe** speed.

**Use speed safely**

Know your limits and keep within the speed at which you feel safe and comfortable – resist the pressures that might encourage you to drive faster.

Remember that at 30 mph a minor misjudgement can be corrected but at 70 mph the same mistake could be disastrous.

## Zones of visibility

The road around you is made up of different zones of visibility. In some areas your view will be good and in others you will only be able to see what is immediately in front of you.

On the approach to a hazard where the view is restricted, use every opportunity to get more information about the road ahead:

open spaces and breaks in hedges, fences and walls on the approach to a blind junction

a curving row of trees or lamp posts

reflections in shop windows

the angle of approaching headlights

the shadow of an approaching vehicle.

Next time you drive along a familiar route, look for opportunities to use additional sources of information. Look for glimpses of wider views and information from lights and shadows.

## Keep your distance

The closer you are to the vehicle in front the less you will be able to see beyond it, especially if it is a van or lorry. In slow-moving traffic it is better to drop back slightly so that you can see what is happening two to three vehicles in front.

You particularly need a good view of the road ahead on motorways and other fast-moving roads. Your view will depend on the curvature and gradient of the carriageway, the lane that you are in, the size and position of other vehicles and the height of your own vehicle. Allowing for these, keep back far enough from the vehicle in front to maintain a safe following distance. Don't sit in the blind spot of other vehicles.

Always check that no one is sitting in your own blind spot before you change lanes. Make sure you know where the offside and nearside blind spots are on any vehicle that you drive. If you're not sure, get a colleague to help you to work this out before you make a journey.

See Chapter 10, *Driving on motorways and multi-lane carriageways.*

When you are following a large lorry keep well back and take views to both sides of it.

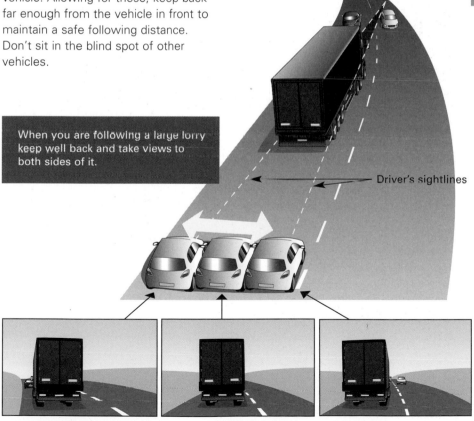

Driver's sightlines

**How well do you anticipate?**

- Think about the last time you misjudged a situation. Did this happen because you failed to observe a hazard? Or did you see the developing hazard but fail to interpret it correctly?

- Did any other factors affect your ability to observe and anticipate? (For example, tiredness, pressure, night driving, bad weather, thinking about the reason for your journey?)

- Can you use your mistake to improve your anticipation in future?

# Physiological factors that affect observation and anticipation

Safe driving is about more than handling your vehicle and the immediate traffic situation. In Chapter 1 you saw why expanding your higher mental skills can improve your driving ability. We also explained some of the psychological, physiological and emotional factors that can affect your driving. Here we look in more detail at the factors that affect observation and anticipation.

## Alertness and tiredness

To anticipate hazards we need to remain alert – ready to identify and respond to constantly changing driving conditions. Alertness determines the amount of information your brain can process. It depends on many things, but with routine tasks like driving it tends to decrease with time spent on the task. Most driving is routine and places few demands on our abilities. This relatively low level of stimulation makes it easy to lose concentration, so you need to take active steps to maintain it, especially on long journeys on motorways or rural roads.

Alertness is reduced if you drive at times when you would normally be asleep or if you have not had a normal amount of sleep. It also varies with the time of day:

- our reactions tend to be slightly faster in the early evening than in the morning

- there seems to be a dip in alertness after the midday meal

- the greatest risk of tiredness-related accidents is between the hours of midnight and 8.00 a.m.

Irregular work and shift patterns also increase the risk of tiredness by disrupting the body's biorhythms or 'biological clock'. This equips your body to perform most tasks by day; at night the relevant brain functions are damped down to allow recuperation and renewal of the body's reserves. Disturbed sleep patterns adversely affect the brain's ability to process information during complex driving tasks.

The ultimate loss in alertness is falling asleep at the wheel; this is a significant cause of motorway accidents. Professional drivers need to be aware that tiredness is related to the total time spent at work and not just to the time spent at the wheel. If you are tired from other duties before you start a journey, you are much more at risk from tiredness during the journey. Tiredness is a particular problem for professional drivers because the demands of the job may mean that they have to drive beyond their safety limit.

## Monotonous conditions

Driving for long periods of time in monotonous conditions such as low-density traffic, fog, at night or on a motorway reduces stimulation and promotes tiredness (see 'Night driving' below). Most people experience some tiredness, whatever the conditions, if they drive for longer than about four hours.

## Practical steps to combat tiredness

The demands of the job and shiftwork mean that police drivers have to learn to deal with tiredness. Watch out for the warning signs such as yawning or loss of concentration and take steps to deal with them well before they become dangerous.

- Adjust your seat so that your driving position is comfortable. Bad posture causes muscular tiredness which in turn causes mental tiredness. This can be a problem during emergency driving when some

drivers become physically tense. If you can, try to relax your posture during emergency driving.

- Noise and vibration cause tiredness, so do everything possible to reduce noise in the vehicle. Keep windows closed and use the ventilation controls instead, but make sure that you have enough ventilation to stay alert.

- Take regular breaks – every two hours if possible – don't wait until you feel drowsy. Most people need a rest break of at least 20 minutes to restore alertness.

- Have a caffeine drink (e.g. coffee or an 'energy' drink) – this needs 15 minutes to take effect.

- On long journeys plan a series of rest breaks, but recognise that each successive break will give less recovery than the one before. Try to include some walking in your breaks. Drivers over 45 are more at risk of, and recover less quickly from, tiredness than younger drivers.

*If you know you are tired, allow yourself a greater safety margin – slow down and be aware you need more time to react.*

In the following pages we look at possible hazards arising out of particular traffic situations. The aim is to 'pre-sensitise' your awareness so that when you encounter a situation you already know what hazards to look for and can react to them more quickly.

# Night driving

When driving at night, you will need to think about:

- your physiological and mental responses to night-time conditions
- how the condition of your vehicle and information in the environment can help you.

Observing in night conditions (anything less than full daylight) is more difficult and yields less information. As the light dwindles, your ability to see the road ahead declines – contrast falls, colours fade and edges become indistinct. Your body naturally wants to slow down as night draws on and you are more likely to grow tired.

Night driving puts extra strain on your eyes. Any slight eyesight irregularity can cause stress and tiredness so if you find you are unexpectedly suffering from tiredness, especially at night, get your eyes tested as soon as possible.

Think about the condition of your vehicle. Windows, mirrors, and the lenses of lights and indicators should all be clean to give the best possible visibility. The slightest film of moisture, grease or dirt on windows or mirrors will break up light and increase glare, making it harder to distinguish what is going on. The lights should be correctly aligned, and adjusted for the vehicle load. The bulbs should all work and the switching equipment should function properly. Windscreen washers, wipers and demisters should also be working properly.

See Know your vehicle, page 164.

## Lights

On unlit roads put your headlights on main beam and only dip them for other road users.

Use dipped headlights:

- in built-up areas
- in situations when dipped headlights are more effective than the main beam, for example when going round a left-hand bend or at a hump back bridge
- in heavy rain, snow and fog when the falling droplets reflect glare from headlights on full beam.

Dip your headlights to avoid dazzling oncoming drivers, the driver in front or other road users. When you overtake another vehicle, return to full beam when you are parallel with it.

Fog lights should only be used when visibility is 100 metres or less.

Always drive so that you can stop safely within the distance you can see to be clear; at night this is the area lit by your headlights unless there is full street lighting. Even in the best conditions your ability to assess the speed and position of oncoming vehicles is reduced at night, so you need to allow an extra safety margin.

## Dazzle

Headlights shining directly into your eyes may dazzle you. This can happen on sharp right-hand bends and steep inclines, and when the lights of oncoming vehicles are undipped or badly adjusted. The intensity of the light bleaches the retinas of your eyes so that you can see nothing for some moments.

To avoid dazzle, look towards the nearside edge of the road. This enables you to keep your road position but does not tell you what is happening in the road ahead, so slow down or stop if necessary. If you are dazzled by undipped headlights, flash your own lights quickly to alert the other driver, but don't retaliate by putting on your full beam. If you did, both you and the other driver would be converging blind. If you suffer temporary blindness, stop and wait until your eyes have adjusted.

## Following other vehicles at night

When you follow another vehicle, dip your headlights and leave a long enough gap so that your lights don't dazzle the driver in front. When you overtake, move out early with your headlights still dipped. If you need to warn the other driver that you are there, flash your lights instead of using the horn. When you are alongside the other vehicle return to full beam. If you are overtaken, dip your headlights when the overtaking vehicle draws alongside you and keep them dipped until you can raise them without dazzling the other driver.

## Information from other vehicles' lights

You can get a great deal of useful information from the front and rear lights of other vehicles; for example, the sweep of the headlights of vehicles ahead approaching a bend can indicate the sharpness of the bend, and the brakelights of vehicles in front can give you an early warning to reduce speed.

Intelligent use of information given by lights can help your driving.

## Reflective studs and markings

Reflective studs and markings are a good source of information about road layout at night. To get the most out of them you need to be familiar with the *Highway Code*. Roadside marker posts reflect your headlights and show you the direction of a curve before you can see where the actual road goes.

## Cat's eyes

Cat's eyes indicate the type of white line along the centre of the road. Generally the more white paint in the line, the greater the number of cat's eyes. They are particularly helpful when it is raining at night and the glare of headlights makes it difficult to see.

## Other ways to improve observation at night

- Keep your speed down when you leave brightly lit areas to allow time for your eyes to adjust to the lower level of lighting.

- Any light inside the vehicle which reflects off the windows will distract you and reduce your ability to see. Interior lights, torches, rally lights and cigarette lighters can cause reflections, so limit their use.

- Certain types of spectacles – such as those with tinted or photochromatic lenses – may be unsuitable for night driving, so check with your optician.

Centre lines:
one cat's eye every other gap.

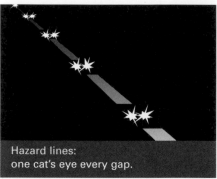

Hazard lines:
one cat's eye every gap.

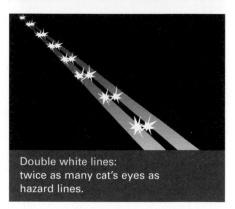

Double white lines:
twice as many cat's eyes as hazard lines.

# Weather conditions

Bad weather is often blamed for causing collisions when the real cause is inappropriate driving. Careful observation, good anticipation, the correct speed and adequate braking distances are crucial for safe driving in difficult weather conditions.

The weather affects how far you can see, and how your vehicle performs, so it is central to your observation, anticipation and driving plan. When weather conditions reduce visibility, reduce your speed and regularly check your actual speed on the speedometer. You should always be able to stop within the distance you can see to be clear. If it is foggy, follow the *Highway Code* fog code. In extreme conditions, consider whether your journey is really necessary.

Examples of weather conditions which reduce visibility are:

- **fog and mist**
- **heavy rain**
- **snow and sleet**
- **bright sunshine**, especially when it is low in the sky.

## Using lights in bad weather

Choose your lights according to the circumstances.

- Switch on your dipped headlights when visibility is poor in daylight or fading light. Use dipped headlights in fog or heavy rain in daylight, because sidelights are virtually invisible.

- As a general rule, use your dipped headlights whenever your wipers are in constant use.

- When there is fog or falling snow at night, foglights often give a better view than dipped headlights. Use them as an alternative to or together with dipped headlights if visibility is 100 metres or less.

- Switch off your foglights when you leave the fog in order not to dazzle other drivers.

- Do not use your main headlight beam when you are behind another vehicle in fog – it may dazzle the driver, and will cast a shadow of the vehicle on the fog ahead, disrupting the driver's view.

- The brightness of rear foglights can mask the brakelights – allow more distance between you and the car in front and aim to brake gently yourself.

## Using auxiliary controls and instruments in bad weather

Make full use of your washers and wipers to keep your windscreen and rear window as clear as possible. When there is a possibility of freezing fog, put freeze-resistant screen wash in the screen wash reservoir. In fog, rain, or snow regularly check your speedometer for your actual speed; you cannot rely on your eyes to judge speed accurately in these conditions. Low visibility distorts your perception of speed.

## Observing when visibility is low

When visibility is low, keep to a slow steady pace and use the edge of the carriageway, hazard lines and cat's eyes as a guide, especially when approaching a road junction or corner. Staring into featureless mist tires the eyes very quickly. Focus instead on what you can see: the vehicle in front, the edge of the road or the road ahead. But avoid fixing your focus on the tail lights of the vehicle in front because they will tend to draw you towards it and you could collide if the vehicle stopped suddenly. Be ready to use your horn to tell other road users you are there.

Always be prepared for a sudden stop in the traffic ahead. Do not follow closely, and only overtake other traffic when you can see that it is absolutely safe to do so. This is seldom possible in fog on a two-way road. At junctions when visibility is low, wind down your window and listen for other vehicles, and consider using your horn.

## Micro climates

Look out for micro climates which can cause frost and wet patches to linger in some areas after they have disappeared elsewhere. Ice can linger in landscape features such as valley bottoms, shaded hillsides and shaded slopes, or large areas of shadow cast by trees or buildings, and result in sudden skidding. Bridge surfaces are often colder than the surrounding roads because they are exposed on all sides, and can be icy when nearby roads are not. Patchy fog is particularly dangerous and is a common cause of multiple collisions.

Ice and wetness can linger in areas of shadow.

# Road surface

The type and condition of the road surface affects tyre grip and vehicle handling characteristics. Tyre grip is fundamental to driving control because it determines steering, acceleration and braking. Most drivers do not pay enough attention to this.

Always look well ahead to identify changes in the road surface, and adjust the strength of your braking, acceleration and steering to retain adequate road holding.

Always observe the camber of the road on a curve or bend.

See Chapter 8, *Cornering*, page 121, Camber and superelevation.

The surfaces of most roads are good for road holding when they are clean and dry. Snow, frost, ice, rain, oil, moist muddy patches, wet leaves, dry loose dust or gravel can cause tyres to lose grip, making skids and aquaplaning more likely. Rain may produce a slippery road surface, especially after a long dry spell. At hazards such as roundabouts or junctions, tyre deposit and diesel spillage may make the surface slippery at precisely the point where effective steering, braking and acceleration are needed to negotiate the hazard safely.

## Road surface irregularities

Look out for irregularities in the road surface such as potholes, projecting manhole covers, sunken gullies and bits of debris, which can damage the tyres and suspension. If you can alter your road position to avoid them without endangering other traffic, do so. If you cannot, slow down to reduce shock and maintain stability as you pass over them.

Surfaces which slope downwards to the inside of the curve help cornering.

Surfaces which slope upwards to the inside of the curve make cornering more difficult.

# The road surface in winter

In winter, the ice or frost covering on road surfaces is not always uniform. Isolated patches remain iced up when other parts have thawed out, and certain slopes are especially susceptible to this. Be on the look out for ice or frost patches, which you can detect by their appearance, by the behaviour of other vehicles and by the sudden absence of tyre noise: tyres travelling on ice make virtually no noise. Adjust your driving early to avoid skidding.

See Chapter 5, *Maintaining vehicle stability.*

| Surfacing materials | Grip characteristics | Problems |
| --- | --- | --- |
| Tarmac or asphalt | Tarmac or asphalt surfaces give a good grip when they are dressed with stones or chips. | In time they become polished and lose some of their skid resistant properties. |
| Anti-skid surface | A high grip anti-skid surface (known as 'shell grip') designed to give extra grip on the approach to fixed hazards such as round-abouts, traffic lights and zebra crossings. | When newly laid, loose gravel on surface can reduce grip; patches can become polished over time. |
| Concrete | Concrete road surfaces often have roughened ribs which give a good skid resistant surface. | Some hold water, which freezes in cold weather and creates a slippery surface which is not easily seen. |
| Cobbles | Low grip when wet. | Rain increases the likelihood of skidding. |

# Driving through water

Driving at speed through water can sharply deflect the front wheels and cause you to lose control. Take extra care at night, when it is difficult to distinguish between a wet road surface and flood water. Flood water can gather quickly where the road dips and at the sides of the road in poorly drained low lying areas. Dips often occur under bridges.

Slow down as you approach a flooded area. Avoid driving through water wherever possible. When you have to drive through water, drive through the shallowest part but look out for hidden obstacles or subsidence.

If the road is entirely submerged, stop the vehicle in a safe place and cautiously find out how deep the water is. The depth of water that you can safely drive through depends on how high your vehicle stands off the ground and where the electrical components, engine, air intake and exhaust pipe are positioned. For example, submerging a hot catalytic converter could cause damage.

Refer to the manufacturer's handbook for specific advice for your vehicle.

If you decide to drive on, follow the steps below:

- Engage first gear and keep the engine running at just above idle speed. (Just enough to prevent stalling).

  (In older vehicles, driving at high revs could prevent water being drawn into the exhaust system. In many newer vehicles, the air intake is positioned below the front bumper so avoid high revs as this would cause water to be sucked into the engine causing expensive damage.)

- Drive through the water at a slow and even speed (a slow walking pace) to avoid making a bow wave.

- Grip the steering wheel more tightly to maintain direction as you drive through the water.

- When you leave the water continue driving slowly and apply the foot brake lightly until the brakes grip. Repeat this again after a short while until you are confident that your brakes are working normally.

If just one wheel enters a deep puddle (usually the nearside wheel), that wheel will slow rapidly causing the vehicle to veer in that direction. If you can't avoid the puddle, prepare by tightening your grip on the steering wheel and holding it straight until clear.

Observation and anticipation

# Road signs and markings

Road signs and markings warn of approaching hazards and give instructions and information about road use.

On road signs the furthest hazard is shown at the bottom and the nearest at the top.

Use your own observations to link the signs to the road layout ahead. Consider the furthest hazard first, so that you observe from the far distance, through the middle ground to the foreground.

Make the best possible use of road signs and markings:

- **Observe** – actively search for road signs and markings in your observation scans, and incorporate the information they give you into your driving plan as soon as possible. Many drivers fail to see and make use of them, and so lose valuable information.

- **Understand** – be able to recognise them immediately. You should be familiar with the *current* edition of the *Highway Code* and *Know your Traffic Signs*.

- **React** – react to a sign or marking by looking ahead to what it refers to and building the information into your driving plan. Where the sign or marking refers to an unseen hazard, anticipate the hazard and adapt your plan accordingly.

**When was the last time you looked at road signs in the current _Highway Code_?**

On your next few journeys, check whether you know the meaning of each sign or road marking you meet and map them against the road layout ahead.

Unofficial road signs such as 'Mud on Road', 'Car Boot Sale' and 'Concealed Entrance' can also help you anticipate the road conditions ahead.

# Local road knowledge

Increasing your local knowledge of the roads can help your driving, but never take familiar roads for granted. Loss of attention is a major cause of collisions and drivers are least attentive on roads they know well. Nine out of ten crashes occur on a road that the driver is familiar with.

Town driving puts heavy demands on your observation, reactions and driving skills, and you need to be alert at all times. At complicated junctions, where it is important to get into the correct lane, local knowledge is useful. But even when you know the layout of main road junctions, one-way streets, roundabouts and other local features, always plan on the basis of what you can actually see – not what usually happens.

# Making observation links

Observation links are clues to the likely behaviour of other road users. Aim to build up your own stock of observation links, which will help you to anticipate road and traffic conditions as you scan the environment.

On the right are some examples of observation links.

## Observation links

When you see a cluster of lamp posts look out for a probable roundabout ahead.

When you see a single lamp post on its own, look out for the exit point of a junction.

When you see no gap in a bank of trees ahead look out for the road to curve to the left or right.

## Some more observation links

| When you see... | Look out for... |
|---|---|
| Railway line beside road | Road will invariably go over or under it, often with sharp turns. |
| A row of parked vehicles | Doors opening, vehicles moving off. Pedestrians stepping out from behind vehicles. Small children hidden from view. |
| A bus at a stop | Pedestrians crossing the road to and from the bus. Bus moving off, possibly at an angle. |
| Pedal cyclists | Inexperienced cyclist doing something erratic. Cyclist looking over shoulder with the intention of turning right. Strong winds causing wobble. Young cyclist doing something dangerous. |

**Practise using observation links. What would you look out for if you observed:**

- a pedestrian calling a cab
- fresh mud on the road
- a courier van
- a catering van or ice cream van in a lay-by
- a motorway slip road
- new hedge clippings or grass cuttings on a narrow country road
- a sign for a large leisure complex?

Can you think of a recent occasion where you failed to spot the significance of something you observed?

Could you use this experience to improve your anticipation skills?

# Review

**In this chapter we have looked at:**

- how you can develop observation and anticipation skills that will help to improve your driving
- the link between observation, planning and acting, and the need to anticipate and prioritise hazards
- how you can extract the fullest meaning from your observations
- why it is important to keep alert and acknowledge tiredness when driving
- using scanning and your peripheral vision to get the maximum information from observation
- how speed affects your ability to observe and anticipate
- using additional sources of information when your view is restricted
- ways of improving observation when you are driving at night
- weather conditions to watch out for and how to adjust your driving to poor visibility
- why you should make full use of information from road signs and markings
- ways to develop your skill at making observation links.

### Check your understanding

Why is anticipation vital to better driving?

What is the relationship between observation and anticipation?

Why do you need a plan and what are the three key stages of planning?

Describe two ways in which you can improve your observation.

How can you get more information when your view is restricted?

In what ways does speed affect your ability to observe your environment?

When should you use dipped headlights?

What hazards should you look out for on the road surface?

Describe at least three examples of observation links.

If you have difficulty in answering any of these questions, look back over the relevant part of this chapter to refresh your memory.

# Chapter 3
# The system of car control

**Use this chapter to find out about:**

- how to use the system of car control
- how to apply the system to common hazards.

This chapter explains the system of car control used in police driver training and outlines the tactical knowledge and skills that will enhance your ability to master a wide range of traffic situations.

# The need for a system of car control

Driver error is a feature of nearly all collisions on the road. The system of car control aims to prevent collisions by providing a systematic approach to hazards. It is a decision-making process that enables you to efficiently handle and act on information that is continuously changing as you drive. Using the system gives you more time to react, which is vital in complex and demanding driving situations.

If you use the system consistently with the thinking, observation and anticipation skills discussed in Chapters 1 and 2, it will help you anticipate dangers caused by other road users and avoid collisions. Your progress will be steady and unobtrusive – the sign of a skilful driver.

## Driving skills and knowledge

As you saw in Chapters 1 and 2, driving requires more than just the ability to handle your vehicle. Developing your understanding of traffic situations and your ability to read the road – the 'situational awareness' skills explored in Chapters 1 and 2 – is essential. Many hazards that drivers meet are unpredictable and the system gives you a methodical way of applying thinking, observation and anticipation skills, so that you can recognise and negotiate hazards safely.

See Chapter 1, *Mental skills for better driving*, and Chapter 2, *Observation and anticipation*.

**Strategic skills**
Taking into account personal factors and attitudes and the goals of the journey that might influence your driving behaviour.

**Tactical skills**
Scanning the environment, recognising, anticipating and prioritising hazards and forming an achievable driving plan.

**Operational skills**
Translating intentions and thoughts into physical action – manoeuvring your vehicle accurately and smoothly.

# What is the system of car control?

The system of car control is a way of approaching and negotiating hazards that is methodical, safe and leaves nothing to chance. It involves careful observation, early anticipation and planning and a systematic use of the controls to maintain your vehicle's stability in all situations.

Driving hazards fluctuate: they come singly and in clusters, they overlap and change all the time. The system takes account of this continual flux because:

- it has a centrally flexible element – you, the driver

- it draws together all levels of driving skill into a logical sequence of actions to help you deal with hazards and respond to new ones safely and efficiently.

In using these skills you need to take into account:

- your driving abilities and limitations

- the behaviour of other road users

- the prevailing weather and road conditions

- the capabilities of the vehicle.

The system of car control is a simple and consistent approach to dealing with a constantly changing driving environment. The system increases your safety by giving you time to react to hazards.

*A hazard is anything which is an actual or potential danger*

See Chapter 2, *Observation and anticipation*, page 20.

## How the system works

The system of car control consists of processing information and four phases – **position, speed, gear** and **acceleration**. Each phase develops out of the one before.

Information is central to the system – it runs through and feeds into all the phases. Start by asking:

- *what information do I need to gather about the road conditions, the behaviour of other road users and actual and potential dangers?*

- *what do other road users need to know about my intentions?*

Then work through each of the phases in turn. As road conditions change, you'll need to process new information

and this will mean re-entering the system at an appropriate point, then continuing through it in sequence. If a new hazard arises, reapply the system and consider all the phases in sequence.

See this chapter, pages 52–57 and Chapter 9, *Overtaking*, page 136 for examples of this principle.

## The importance of information

In Chapter 1 you saw how the brain processes information and how your ability to process information is essential to becoming a better driver.

See Chapter 1, *Mental skills for better driving.*

Processing information (taking, using and giving information) introduces the system and continues throughout.

## Information

**Position** **Speed** **Gear** **Acceleration**

*Taking, using and giving **information** is the process on which the other phases – **position, speed, gear, acceleration** – depend.*

You need to:

- **take and use information** to plan your driving
- **give information** whenever other road users could benefit from it.

Develop your skill at assessing the continuous flow of information. This skill underpins the entire system and enables you to adapt it to changes in road circumstances.

See Chapter 6, *Driver's signals.*

## Taking and giving information: mirrors and signals

- Take information:
  Whenever you consider changing position or speed, always check first what is happening to the front, sides and behind you. You must check your mirrors at this point.

- Give information:
  Signal whenever it could benefit another road user.

- Give information:
  Sound your horn when you think another road user could benefit. Its purpose is to tell other people you are there – not to rebuke them.

## Information

### Position — Speed — Gear — Acceleration

# The system of car control

The system of car control is set out in detail here. Use this information in conjunction with the other chapters in *Roadcraft* for a complete understanding of the system. When and how you read each chapter depends on your own study plan. If you are using *Roadcraft* as part of a course, ask your instructor for advice.

## Information

Processing information runs throughout all phases of the system.

### Take information

Look all round you. Scan to the front and sides. Use your mirrors at appropriate points in the system.

See Chapter 2, *Observation and anticipation.*

### Use information

Use information to plan how to deal with the hazards you identify. Use the system to decide on your next action. If new hazards arise, consider whether to re-run the system from an earlier phase.

See Chapter 2, *Observation and anticipation,* page 21, Planning.

### Give information

Give a signal if it could help other road users – including pedestrians and cyclists: use indicators, the horn or flash your lights. The earlier your warning signal, the greater the benefit.

Be aware that the position of your vehicle gives valuable information to other road users.

See Chapter 6, *Driver's signals.*

## Position

Position yourself so that you can pass the hazard(s) safely and smoothly.

See Chapter 7, *Positioning.*

Take account of other road users, including pedestrians, cyclists and children.

## Speed

Adjust your speed as necessary.
Use the accelerator or brake to give you the correct speed to complete the manoeuvre safely. Make good use of acceleration sense.

See Chapter 4, *Acceleration, using gears, braking and steering.*

Use your anticipation skills so that you make all adjustments in speed smoothly and steadily.

## Gear

Once you have the correct speed for the circumstances, engage the appropriate gear for that speed.

See Chapter 4, *Acceleration, using gears, braking and steering*, page 66.

*Brake/gear overlap should only be used in specific circumstances. It must be part of a planned approach that is the most appropriate for the circumstances. Please turn to Chapter 4 page 69 for a full discussion of this point.*

## Acceleration

Apply the correct degree of acceleration to negotiate and leave the hazard safely. Use the accelerator to maintain speed and stability through the hazard. Depress the accelerator sufficiently to offset any loss of speed due to cornering forces.

Taking account of your speed, other road users, and the road and traffic conditions ahead, decide whether it is appropriate to accelerate away from the hazard.

Choose an appropriate point to accelerate safely and smoothly away from the hazard; adjust acceleration to the circumstances.

See Chapter 4, *Acceleration,using gears, braking and steering*, page 62.

---

*Continuously assessing information runs through every phase of the system*

# Use the system flexibly

The system works if you use it intelligently and proactively and adapt it to circumstances as they arise:

- consider all phases of the system on the approach to every hazard, but you may not need to use every phase in a particular situation

- take, use and give information throughout to constantly reassess your plans

- be ready to return to an earlier phase of the system as new hazards arise.

With practice, the system will become second nature and form a sound basis for developing the finer points of your driving skill. It will help you process information, make decisions and plan your approach to hazards so that you are able to avoid or give yourself plenty of time to react to potential dangers.

See Chapter 1, *Mental skills for better driving*, page 4.

---

**Applying the system**

When you begin using the system, it may help to name each phase out loud as you enter it. After you practise using the system, review your performance:

- **Do you take, use and give information throughout all phases?**

- **Do you consider each phase?**

- **Do you think about all aspects of each phase?**

- **Do you work systematically through the phases?**

Where you have identified problems in using the system, work through them one by one, solving the first before you go on to the next.

Also think about mental factors that might create difficulties in using the system, such as anxiety or tiredness. If the purpose of a particular journey is likely to distract you, consider making a running commentary to help you to focus on working through the system.

We now look at how you can apply the system to four common hazards: a right-hand turn, a left-hand turn, a roundabout and a child on the pavement. (Before looking at these examples, make sure you know thoroughly the *Highway Code* advice on road junctions and roundabouts.)

## Applying the system to a right-hand turn

### Information

Use your mirrors throughout. Look to the front and sides to know the position and anticipate the intentions of other road users. Give a signal at any point where this could help other road users – including pedestrians and cyclists.

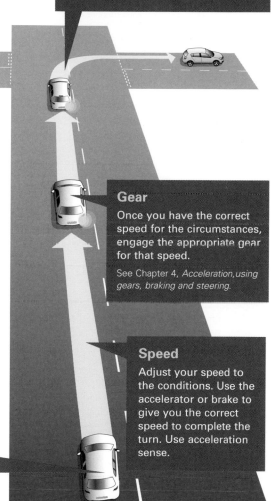

### Acceleration

Depress the accelerator to maintain road speed round the corner. Choose the appropriate point to accelerate safely and smoothly away from the hazard, paying attention to the amount of acceleration, the nature of the road and road surface, traffic conditions ahead, and the position and movement of other road users.

*See Chapter 4, Acceleration, using gears, braking and steering.*

### Gear

Once you have the correct speed for the circumstances, engage the appropriate gear for that speed.

*See Chapter 4, Acceleration, using gears, braking and steering.*

### Speed

Adjust your speed to the conditions. Use the accelerator or brake to give you the correct speed to complete the turn. Use acceleration sense.

### Position

Alter your position to make the turn in good time. The usual position would be towards the centre of the road, but think about:

- the width of the road
- lane markings
- hazards in the road
- the speed, size and position of other vehicles
- the flow of traffic behind you
- getting a good view
- making your intentions clear to other road users.

# Applying the system to a left-hand turn

## Information

Use your mirrors throughout. Look to the front and sides to know the position and anticipate the intentions of other road users. Give a signal at any point where this could help other road users – including pedestrians and cyclists.

### Acceleration

Depress the accelerator to maintain road speed round the corner. Choose the appropriate point to accelerate safely and smoothly away from the hazard, paying attention to the amount of acceleration, the nature of the road and road surface, traffic conditions ahead, and the position and movement of other road users.

See Chapter 4, page 64 for more information about accelerating out of a bend.

*Know what is going on all around you, and let other road users know what you intend to do. You must take, use and give information before you change speed or direction.*

### Gear

Once you have the correct speed for the circumstances, engage the appropriate gear for that speed.

See Chapter 4 page 69 for further discussion of braking and gear changing on a left-hand turn.

### Speed

Adjust your speed to the conditions. Use the accelerator or brake to give you the correct speed to complete the turn. Use acceleration sense.

Generally a left turn is slower than a right because the turning arc is tighter.

### Position

Take a position towards the left of the road. Adapt to the road and traffic conditions.

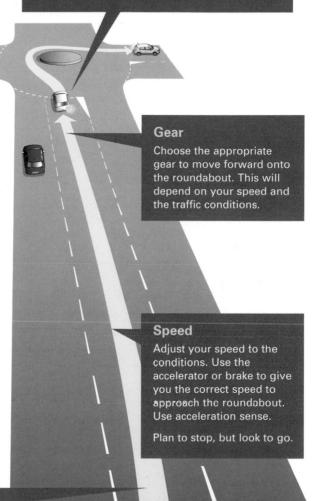

## Applying the system to a roundabout

### Information

Identify hazards. Scan to the front, sides and rear. Use your mirrors and consider a shoulder check.

Decide early which exit to take and in which lane to approach the roundabout.

Give a signal when it could benefit other road users.

Take an early view of traffic on the roundabout and approaching it from other entrances.

As you approach the roundabout be prepared to stop, but look for your opportunity to go.

### Acceleration

Choose an appropriate gap in the traffic to accelerate safely and smoothly onto the roundabout without disrupting traffic already using it. When you are on the roundabout, deal with any new hazards using the appropriate phases of the system.

### Gear

Choose the appropriate gear to move forward onto the roundabout. This will depend on your speed and the traffic conditions.

### Speed

Adjust your speed to the conditions. Use the accelerator or brake to give you the correct speed to approach the roundabout. Use acceleration sense.

Plan to stop, but look to go.

### Position

Your approach position will depend on your intended exit and the number of approach lanes.

The system of car control

# Reapplying the system to leave the roundabout

## Information

As you leave the roundabout, reapply the system. Plan the appropriate lane for your exit. If you need to move into the left-hand lane, check that your nearside road space is clear. Use your nearside mirror and check your blind spot. Signal left if it could benefit other road users.

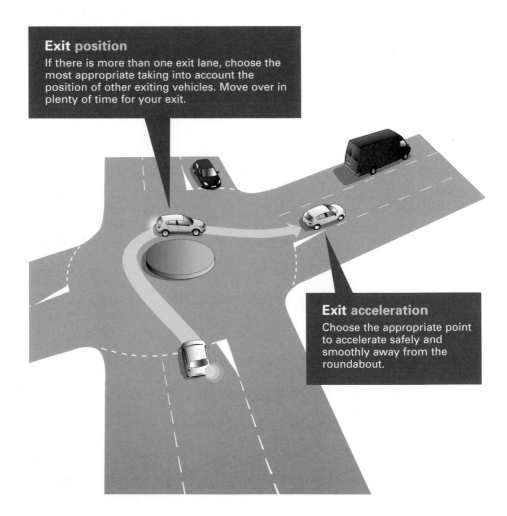

**Exit position**
If there is more than one exit lane, choose the most appropriate taking into account the position of other exiting vehicles. Move over in plenty of time for your exit.

**Exit acceleration**
Choose the appropriate point to accelerate safely and smoothly away from the roundabout.

## Applying the system
## to a footpath hazard

### Information

Use your mirrors throughout. Look to the front and sides to know the position and anticipate the intentions of other road users. Give a signal at any point where this could help other road users – including pedestrians and cyclists.

**Acceleration**

Accelerate *safely* and smoothly away once you have passed the hazard.

**Gear**

Once you have the correct speed for the circumstances, engage the appropriate gear for that speed.

**Speed**

Use the brake to reduce your speed so you can stop safely if the children step into the road.

**Position**

Take a position towards the centre of the road in case a child steps out. Adapt to the road and traffic conditions.

# Review

**In this chapter we have looked at:**

- the system of car control
- applying the system to some common hazards.

## Check your understanding

What is a hazard?

How does the system of car control increase the safety of your driving?

What are the elements of the system of car control?

Which is the central part of the system and why?

What are the main ways in which you can give information to other road users?

When should you consider giving a signal?

How should you decide which gear to select?

Why is it vital to use the system flexibly?

If you have difficulty in answering any of these questions, look back over the relevant part of this chapter to refresh your memory.

# Chapter 4
# Acceleration, using gears, braking and steering

**Use this chapter to find out about:**

- tyre grip
- vehicle balance
- accelerating
- using the gears
- braking
- steering.

# Developing your skill at controlling your vehicle

The aim of this chapter is to give you complete control over moving, stopping and changing the direction of your vehicle at all times. To achieve this level of skill, you need to understand in detail how the accelerator, gears, brakes and steering controls work and how to make best use of them.

*A moving vehicle is most stable when its weight is evenly distributed, its engine is just pulling without increasing road speed, and it is travelling in a straight line.*

Control of your vehicle and your own and others' safety depends on the grip between your tyres and the road.

## The tyre grip trade-off

There is a limited amount of tyre grip available. The patch of tyre in contact with the road is about the same area as a CD cover. This is shared between accelerating, braking and steering forces. If more tyre grip is used for braking or accelerating, there is less available for steering, and vice versa.

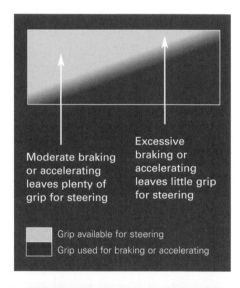

Moderate braking or accelerating leaves plenty of grip for steering

Excessive braking or accelerating leaves little grip for steering

Grip available for steering

Grip used for braking or accelerating

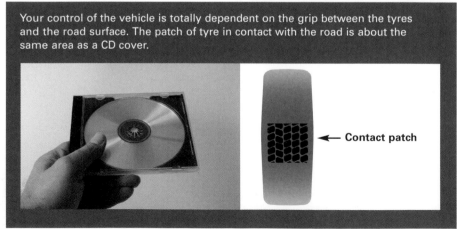

Your control of the vehicle is totally dependent on the grip between the tyres and the road surface. The patch of tyre in contact with the road is about the same area as a CD cover.

← Contact patch

# Vehicle balance and tyre grip

Tyre grip is not necessarily the same on each wheel. It varies with the load on the wheel and this affects how the vehicle handles. Braking, steering and accelerating alter the distribution of the load between the wheels and so affect the vehicle's balance.

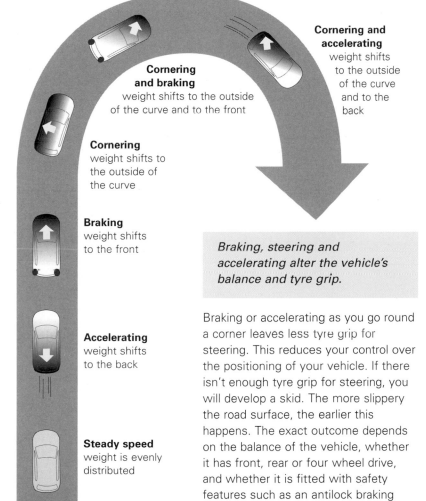

**Cornering and accelerating**
weight shifts to the outside of the curve and to the back

**Cornering and braking**
weight shifts to the outside of the curve and to the front

**Cornering**
weight shifts to the outside of the curve

**Braking**
weight shifts to the front

**Accelerating**
weight shifts to the back

**Steady speed**
weight is evenly distributed

*Braking, steering and accelerating alter the vehicle's balance and tyre grip.*

Braking or accelerating as you go round a corner leaves less tyre grip for steering. This reduces your control over the positioning of your vehicle. If there isn't enough tyre grip for steering, you will develop a skid. The more slippery the road surface, the earlier this happens. The exact outcome depends on the balance of the vehicle, whether it has front, rear or four wheel drive, and whether it is fitted with safety features such as an antilock braking system (ABS), electronic stability control (ESC) or traction control.

## Technology to help keep control of the vehicle

Many vehicles are now fitted with electronic safety features to help the driver keep control of the vehicle when harsh steering, braking or acceleration might result in a skid. These include ABS, traction control and electronic stability control systems. The specific technology and how it works varies from one manufacturer to another. This technology is also developing fast, with increasing sophistication. We look in the next chapter at some of the systems that can help drivers to avoid skidding.

See Chapter 5, *Maintaining vehicle stability*, page 89.

---

**Develop your awareness of tyre grip**

Analyse what is happening to your tyre grip as you steer round a corner or bend.

Be aware of the trade-off between accelerating or braking on the one hand and steering on the other.

- Do you finish braking before you go into a bend?

- Do you avoid accelerating harshly while driving round bends?

---

# Using the accelerator

If you are in the correct gear for your speed, depressing the accelerator will give you a responsive increase in engine speed. If you are in too high a gear, the engine will not respond because the load from the wheels is too great. Changing to a lower gear reduces the load and allows the engine to speed up and move the vehicle faster.

If you release the accelerator pedal you get the opposite effect – deceleration. The engine speed slows down and cylinder compression slows the vehicle down. The lower the gear the greater the slowing effect of the engine. So, in the correct gear, the accelerator pedal has three effects:

- depress the pedal to increase speed

- release the pedal to decrease speed

- gradually ease off pressure on the pedal to gently decrease speed.

## Acceleration and vehicle balance

Acceleration alters the distribution of weight between the wheels of the car. When a vehicle accelerates, the weight is lifted from the front and pushed down on the back wheels. During deceleration the opposite happens. This alters the relative grip of the front and rear tyres.

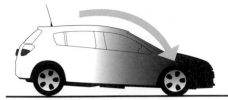

During deceleration
the rear tyres lose grip
the front tyres gain grip

During acceleration
the rear tyres gain grip
the front tyres lose grip

## How acceleration affects different vehicles

Acceleration affects rear wheel drive and most four wheel drive vehicles differently from front wheel drive vehicles.

- **Front wheel drive vehicles** lose grip or traction on their driving wheels because acceleration transfers weight, and therefore grip, from front to back wheels. This reduces their ability to accelerate. Accelerating too sharply causes wheel spin. Harsh acceleration or a slippery road surface increases the risk of wheel spin, which can be particularly dangerous when pulling out at a junction. Avoid accelerating sharply and in slippery conditions depress the accelerator very gently.

- **Rear wheel drive vehicles** gain extra grip on their driving wheels, which helps acceleration (but harsh acceleration will cause the driving wheels to lose traction). At the same time the front is lightened.

- **Four wheel drive vehicles** vary in how the power is divided between the front and back wheels, and in the type of central differential they have. This means the effects of acceleration vary according to the model but generally four wheel drive vehicles have good grip when accelerating. For precise details consult your vehicle manufacturer.

## Develop your skill at using the accelerator

Jerky acceleration is uncomfortable for the passengers, puts unnecessary strains on the vehicle, and adversely affects tyre grip. Use accurate and smooth movements to depress or release the accelerator – squeeze and ease it.

Acceleration capability varies widely between vehicles and depends on the size of the engine, its efficiency, the power-to-weight ratio and its load. Take time to get to know the acceleration capability of any vehicle you drive: the safety of many manoeuvres, particularly overtaking, depends on judging it well.

How you use the accelerator affects your own and other road users' safety. Sudden sharp movements of the accelerator reduce tyre grip and jeopardise steering control. The faster you go the further you will travel before you can react to a hazard. It will take you longer to stop and, if you collide, the results of the impact will be worse.

## Acceleration sense

*Acceleration sense is the ability to vary vehicle speed in response to changing road and traffic conditions by the accurate use of the accelerator.*

You need this in every driving situation: moving off, overtaking, complying with speed limits, following other vehicles and negotiating hazards. Acceleration sense requires careful observation, full anticipation, sound judgement of speed and distance, driving experience and an

**When you come up behind another vehicle, how often do you need to brake to match the speed of the driver in front?**

If your answer is 'always' or 'nearly always' work at developing your acceleration sense.

Drive along a regular route using acceleration sense rather than braking. Notice how it improves your anticipation and increases the smoothness of the drive.

awareness of a particular vehicle's capabilities.

Acceleration sense helps you avoid unnecessary braking. Common mistakes are accelerating hard away from a junction and then having to brake sharply to slow to the speed of the vehicles in front or accelerating to move up behind a slower moving vehicle and then having to brake before overtaking.

## Accelerating on bends

A moving vehicle is most stable when its weight is evenly distributed, its engine is just pulling without increasing road speed, and it is travelling in a straight line.

As soon as a vehicle turns into a bend it starts to slow down and lose stability, due to cornering forces. If you maintain the same accelerator setting as you go into and round a bend, you will lose road speed.

*Maintain a constant speed round a bend to keep your weight evenly distributed front and rear, to ensure maximum tyre grip.*

If you accelerate to increase road speed and you alter direction at the same time you may demand too much from the available tyre grip and risk losing steering control. To retain maximum steering control and stability, aim to keep your road speed constant round the bend.

To maintain constant speed, increase power by depressing the accelerator.

Your aim is not increase your road speed but to keep it steady. How much to depress the accelerator is a matter of judgement and practice.

Increasing road speed on bends reduces vehicle stability. When you need to steer and increase speed together, use the accelerator *gently*. Take extra care when accelerating in slippery conditions or you may cause wheel spin, loss of steering control and a developing skid.

See Chapter 8, *Cornering*, page 119, Cornering forces.

Acceleration reduces the ability to corner because it shifts the vehicle's weight on to the back wheels and reduces front tyre grip. In front wheel drive vehicles there is a risk of wheel spin on the front wheels because they are the driving wheels. Do not make the mistake of applying even more steering which may lead to loss of control.

**Coming out of the bend**

Having passed the apex of the bend, your new road view (**B** – **C**) begins to open rapidly, and is greater than the distance you have travelled (**2** – **3**). It is safe to accelerate smoothly into the straightening road.

**Entering the bend**

Your increased road view (**A** – **B**) is no greater than the distance you have travelled (**1** – **2**) so maintain a constant speed. Increase pressure on the accelerator to maintain but not increase road speed.

**Approaching the bend**

As you approach the bend, adjust your speed so that you can stop within the distance you can see to be clear (**1** – **A**)

*Follow the guiding safety principle – you must always be able to stop safely within the distance you can see to be clear. If that distance shortens, you must slow to match it.*

Acceleration, using gears, braking and steering

## Key points

- The harder your accelerate, the less tyre grip you have for steering.
- Use the accelerator smoothly – jerkiness causes wheel spin.
- Use acceleration sense to vary your road speed without unnecessary braking.

## Power source affects acceleration and engine braking

Diesel, petrol and electric vehicles differ in their acceleration and engine braking characteristics. (Engine braking is discussed in more detail later in this chapter.)

The range of technology built into new vehicles to improve engine performance means that different makes and models with the same type of power source can also have markedly different acceleration or engine braking characteristics. Consult your vehicle handbook for an exact specification and make sure you are familiar with the acceleration and engine braking characteristics of any vehicle you drive.

# Using the gears

Correct use of the gears depends on accurately matching the gear to the road speed, and using the clutch and accelerator precisely. Your vehicle can only increase speed if the engine can deliver the power and it can only do this if you are in the correct gear. Aim to:

- be in the correct gear for every road speed and traffic situation
- make all gear changes smoothly
- engage a chosen gear without going through an intermediate gear first
- know the approximate maximum road speed for each gear of the vehicle.

For economic progress, accelerate up to the engine's peak performance point and then change to a higher gear. Bear in mind the manufacturer's peak engine performance recommendations for your vehicle. This may differ from both the maximum torque (ability of the engine to turn the wheels) and the maximum revs obtainable from the engine.

The main effect of the gears is to transform engine revs into usable power.

- In a low gear, the engine is able to rev more freely, which allows the vehicle to accelerate rapidly and to climb steep slopes.
- In a higher gear, lower revs deliver more speed but less ability to accelerate or to climb slopes.
- Intermediate gears allow progress from one extreme to the other.
- A lower gear also restrains the vehicle's speed when descending a steep slope.

The greater turning power of low gears also affects tyre grip. The greater the turning power, the more likely that the tyres will lose grip. This is why wheel spin occurs when you accelerate hard in first gear.

This is why it is advisable to use a higher gear when moving slowly in slippery conditions such as on snow, ice or mud. When moving off from a standstill on ice, use first gear and slip the clutch without accelerating. You will gain traction and slowly pull forward.

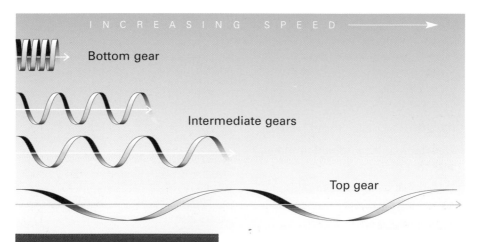

Bottom gear
produces plenty of road wheel turning power but not much speed

Intermediate gears
produce varying combinations of wheel turning power and speed

Top gear
produces plenty of speed but not much wheel turning power

Changing to a lower gear helps when:

- travelling at low speeds
- going uphill
- going downhill, because engine compression slows the descent
- approaching a hazard
- on slippery roads, where you should ease off the accelerator to lose speed gently, so as to avoid skidding.

High gears are good for:

- cruising at speed
- certain slippery conditions where lower gears may cause wheel spin.

## Moving off from stationary

From a standing start, accelerate smoothly and gather speed by steadily working up through the gears. You should only use maximum acceleration through the gears if there is a pressing need, and if the road surface and other conditions are safe. Over-accelerating in low gears or remaining in a gear beyond the limits of its best performance damages the engine, uses excessive fuel and results in slower progress. Some engines cut out or misfire if excessively revved.

### Key points

- Develop good coordination of hand and foot movements.

- Recognise when to change gear by the sound of the engine.

- Choose the correct gear for the road speed.

- Use the brakes rather than engine compression to slow the vehicle (except during hill descents and when there is a risk of skidding).

- Brake in good time to slow to the right road speed as you approach a hazard, and then select the appropriate gear.

- Match engine speed to road speed before you change down.

# Automatic and semi-automatic transmissions

All automatic and semi-automatic transmissions operate and behave differently from manual gearboxes and from each other, so always consult the vehicle handbook.

An automatic transmission changes gear automatically as the vehicle moves, allowing you more time to concentrate on your driving and to keep both hands on the steering wheel for longer. An automatic system has a gear selector on the floor or steering column that allows you to choose the mode you need – typically, Park (**P**), Reverse (**R**), Neutral (**N**), and Drive (**D**). The key points are:

- always ensure that the footbrake is on before engaging either **D** or **R** from stationary

- do not engage **D** or **R** with a high revving engine.

There is an increasing range of transmission technologies to automatically adjust the gear ratio between the engine and the wheels. Some types of automatic transmission allow you to choose different combinations of gear modes. For any vehicle that you drive it is vital that you:

- read the manufacturer's instructions

- know the type of gearbox fitted and how to use it.

# Overlapping braking and gear changing in limited circumstances

The individual phases of the system of car control are almost always applied separately: the fundamental principle is that brakes are to **slow**, gears are to **go**.

In some circumstances it may be helpful to overlap braking with the gear change by braking normally but changing the gear earlier, towards the end of braking.

If you use this technique it must be part of a planned approach to a hazard. Begin applying the system *at the same time and in the same place* as you would normally. The system is not compressed.

When drivers first learn the system of car control, they separate braking and gear changing and try not to overlap. The problem with this approach to tight turns is that if you brake some distance before the turn to avoid an overlap you can confuse other drivers with unexpected results. Following drivers may think you are stopping and be tempted to overtake. Approaching drivers preparing to turn into the same junction may think you have slowed to leave space for them to turn ahead of you.

**Situations where brake/gear overlap may be appropriate:**

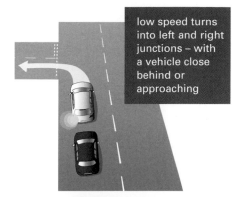

low speed turns into left and right junctions – with a vehicle close behind or approaching

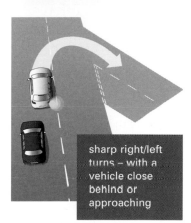

sharp right/left turns – with a vehicle close behind or approaching

going downhill

Acceleration, using gears, braking and steering

## Brake/gear overlap – an example

Here is an example of using brake/gear overlap as a planned approach to a hazard, in order to maintain correct speed.

If you turn left into a side road which is part way down a hill, the vehicle will start to accelerate when you take your foot off the brake. Instead, apply the system as normal up to and including the speed phase.

## Incorrect use of brake/gear overlap

Brake/gear overlap has a bad reputation because it is frequently misused by drivers who approach a hazard too quickly:

- overlap that is not properly planned results in late, excessive braking and rushed gear changes
- braking late and rushing a gear change can destabilise your vehicle at exactly the point where you need greatest stability to negotiate the hazard.

But applied carefully in certain circumstances, brake/gear overlap takes less time.

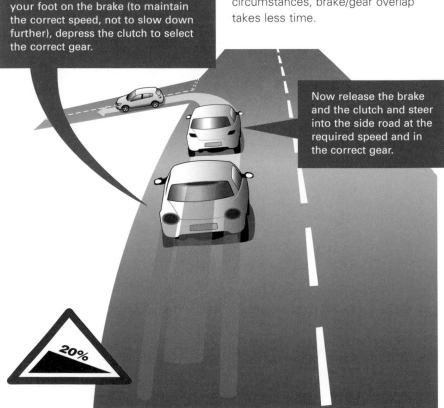

Use the brakes to get the correct speed for the left turn. Then, keeping your foot on the brake (to maintain the correct speed, not to slow down further), depress the clutch to select the correct gear.

Now release the brake and the clutch and steer into the side road at the required speed and in the correct gear.

20%

## How well do you use your gears?

Ask yourself the following questions

- Are you always in the correct gear?

- Do you adjust your speed first, then select the appropriate gear?

- Do you avoid using your gears to slow down except on hills and slippery surfaces?

- Do you ever find yourself changing gear halfway round a corner?

You should avoid changing gear while cornering because it destabilises the vehicle and requires you to take one hand off the steering wheel.

# Slowing down and stopping

You need to be able to slow down or stop smoothly and with your vehicle fully under control. Anticipate the need to slow down or stop early and brake progressively. Being able to accurately estimate the required braking distance at different speeds and in different conditions is central to skilful driving. There are two ways of slowing down (decelerating) or stopping:

- **releasing or easing off the accelerator**

- **using the brakes**.

## Releasing the accelerator (engine braking)

When you release the accelerator the engine slows and through engine compression exerts a slowing force on the wheels. This causes the engine to act as a brake, reducing road speed smoothly and gradually with little wear to the vehicle.

The loss of road speed is greater when you ease off the accelerator in a low gear. (This applies equally to automatic gearboxes.) Engine braking allows you to lose speed in conditions where normal braking might lock the wheels – for example, on slippery roads. It is also useful on long descents in hilly country. In normal driving, though, engine braking can only be used to produce gradual variations in speed.

Acceleration, using gears, braking and steering

## Using the brakes

Use the brakes if you need to make more than a gradual adjustment to your road speed. For maximum control, you should keep both hands on the wheel while you brake, and plan to avoid braking on bends and corners. (But note the discussion on brake/gear overlap earlier.) You can apply pressure to the footbrake to achieve the slightest check or, at the other extreme, until just before the wheels lock up (or the ABS intervenes). Try to avoid locking the wheels completely because this will cause you to lose steering contol. Remember to make allowances for extra loads or changes in road surface.

> *Check the brakes every time you use your vehicle, both before you move off and when the vehicle is moving.*

See Know your vehicle, page 164.

## Normal braking (tapered braking)

Braking should normally be progressive and increased steadily.

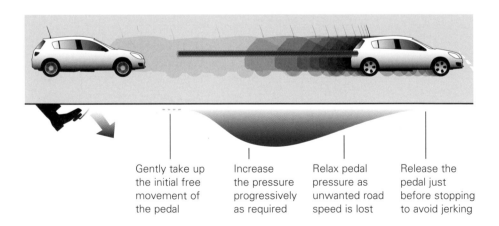

| Gently take up the initial free movement of the pedal | Increase the pressure progressively as required | Relax pedal pressure as unwanted road speed is lost | Release the pedal just before stopping to avoid jerking |

## Braking, tyre grip and balance

Braking moves the weight of the vehicle forward on to the front wheels. This makes the steering heavier and at the same time reduces the grip of the rear tyres. On a bend this reduces stability and can cause a skid. The harsher the braking, the greater the demand on tyre grip and the less your ability to steer. In slippery conditions harsh braking almost inevitably results in a skid.

Braking reduces the grip of the rear tyres. On a bend this unbalances the vehicle.

## The safe stopping distance rule

This is one of the guiding principles of *Roadcraft*. By relating your speed to the distance within which you can stop, you can adopt a safe speed in any situation.

*Never drive so fast that you cannot stop safely within the distance you can see to be clear.*

The importance of observing this rule for your own and other people's safety cannot be overstated. It provides a guide to the speed at which you should corner and the distance you should keep from other vehicles in all other traffic conditions. Successfully applying this rule requires skill. You need to be aware of:

- the braking capabilities of your vehicle
- the type and condition of the road surface – in slippery or wet conditions braking distances increase greatly
- the effects of cornering, braking and vehicle balance on tyre grip.

In narrow and single track lanes, allow twice the overall stopping distance that you can see to be clear to allow room for any oncoming vehicle to brake also.

Acceleration, using gears, braking and steering

# Overall safe stopping distance

To work out the overall safe stopping distance, add thinking distance to braking distance.

Thinking distance + Braking distance = Stopping distance

**Thinking distance** is the distance travelled in the time between first observing the need for action and acting. This is why attitude, observation, anticipation and information-processing abilities are vital.

> *Actual thinking distance varies according to the speed of the vehicle, your physical and mental condition, your attentiveness and whether or not you are expecting something to happen.*

It takes much longer to react to unexpected events than to expected ones – you need less thinking time if you are anticipating events and not just reacting to them.

Some common medicines (e.g. some antihistamines for hay fever) can make you drowsy and slow your thinking and should be used with care.

**Braking distance** is the distance needed for braking. Actual braking distance depends on the vehicle's capability, the gradient of the road and the condition of the road surface – slippery surfaces greatly increase braking distances.

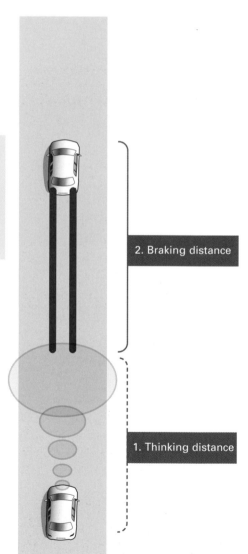

2. Braking distance

1. Thinking distance

## The two-second rule

To keep a safe distance between you and the vehicle in front on fast roads, leave a gap of at least two seconds. But remember your overall stopping distance depends on your speed and the condition of the road surface. An easy way to count two seconds is to say: *Only a fool breaks the two-second rule.*

> **Note when the car in front passes over a mark or shadow on the road.**
>
> Count one second
>
> *A 619*
>
> Count two seconds
>
> **If you pass over the mark or shadow on the road before you have counted two seconds, you are too close. Drop back and try the test again.**

You need to allow at least double this distance in wet weather and even more in icy conditions. If the vehicle behind you is too close, drop back further from the vehicle in front. This will allow you to brake more gently in an emergency and may prevent you being rammed from behind.

## Braking for corners and bends

Braking affects the balance, stability and cornering ability of vehicles, so you need to plan braking carefully for a corner or bend:

- plan to avoid braking on corners because it increases the demand on tyre grip; if braking is necessary, apply the brakes gently and steadily
- brake in plenty of time
- adjust brake pressure to the condition or grip of the road surface
- on steep winding descents brake firmly on the straight stretches and gently on the bends; remember to use a low gear at an early stage in the descent.

## Braking as you approach a hazard

To apply the system of car control, consider your road speed on the approach to a hazard and slow down if necessary. Always check your mirrors before you reduce speed or change direction. Choose the best road position and then reduce speed safely and smoothly using engine braking, braking or a combination of both.

Acceleration, using gears, braking and steering

When and how firmly you apply the brakes depends on your judgement of speed and distance. Consider:

- your initial speed
- the road surface
- weather conditions
- the specific road and traffic conditions.

Sometimes braking may need to be firm but it should never be harsh. Harsh braking usually results from poor observation, anticipation and planning. Aim to lose speed steadily from the first moment until you achieve the correct speed to negotiate the hazard. Timing is crucial: avoid braking so early that you have to re-accelerate to reach the hazard, or so late that you have to brake harshly.

See Chapter 3, *The system of car control*, page 51.

## Emergency braking on a good dry road

The quickest and shortest way to stop on a dry straight road is to brake until the wheels lock up.

**In a vehicle with an antilock braking system (ABS)**, the ABS repeatedly releases the brakes just before the wheels lock up and reapplies them in a pulsing action, so that they never fully lock. ABS only works if you maintain firm pressure on the brake pedal. The advantage of ABS is that it gives you some steering control during emergency braking – see Chapter 5 for a full explanation.

**In an older vehicle without ABS** locking the wheels achieves a high degree of braking but once the wheels are locked all steering effect is lost. You must quickly decide either to brake to a standstill on a straight course, if there is room to do so, or to relax brake pressure to steer out of trouble. In a vehicle without ABS, one option is to use the cadence braking technique described below.

## Cadence braking

If your vehicle has ABS do not do this. Read the manufacturer's handbook.

In a vehicle without ABS, applying the brakes repeatedly gives you some steering control during braking. (This is in effect what ABS does electronically.) Apply the brakes firmly to lock the wheels momentarily and then release

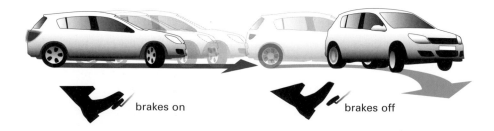

brakes on   brakes off

them to allow the wheels to rotate again, so that you regain steering. Repeat this sequence deliberately and rhythmically until sufficient road speed is lost. Braking occurs while the brakes are on, steering while they are off.

> *ABS and cadence braking do not help **braking** – they help **steering** while braking.*

## Emergency braking on a slippery road

In a vehicle without ABS, cadence braking gives you some steering control when braking on a slippery road. However, it is much better not to have to brake sharply in these conditions. Use your observation and anticipation skills to recognise where slippery conditions are likely, and adjust your speed.

See also Chapter 5, *Maintaining vehicle stability.*

## Using the handbrake

Methods for applying and locking the handbrake vary, so check and follow the manufacturer's instructions.

Only use the handbrake when the vehicle is stationary. New drivers are often taught to use the handbrake every time they come to a standstill on a journey. With experience you can judge whether you need to put the handbrake on for every momentary stop.

# Steering

A well-maintained vehicle travelling along a flat, straight road should hold its position with minimal steering. Camber, crossfall, or side winds can move the vehicle to one side but a small steering adjustment will keep the vehicle on a straight course. Usually you only need to make positive steering adjustments when you alter position or turn the vehicle. Steering characteristics vary between vehicles, so make sure you are familiar with the characteristics of vehicles you drive. Some vehicles respond more than average to steering (oversteer) and others less (understeer). Power assisted steering (PAS) assists steering at slow speeds and may cause you to oversteer if you're not used to it.

## Steering technique

Police driving schools have developed a range of steering techniques to suit different policing situations. The most widely adopted is the pull–push method which provides safe and efficient steering in a wide range of circumstances.

Your steering method should be determined by the control, efficiency and comfort you experience throughout the full range of steering movements. This may vary according to:

- the car you are driving (the lightness of its steering, the diameter of the steering wheel, the castor action and the number of turns from lock to lock)
- how you sit in relation to the steering wheel
- your size and shape.

Acceleration, using gears, braking and steering

## Seat position

Good steering starts with getting your body in the right position in relation to the steering wheel. Adjust the position and angle of your seat so that you can reach the controls comfortably. Aim for a position which allows greatest control of the steering without being uncomfortable. An uncomfortable position will tire you and impair your driving.

You're likely to be in a good sitting position when:

- both hands are on the steering wheel and your elbows are slightly bent

- you can depress the clutch pedal to its full extent and your knee is still slightly bent.

## How to hold the steering wheel

- Place your hands on the wheel with your palms on the rim. Your thumbs should extend out and be placed on the rim so that your thumb nails are towards you.

- Hold the wheel lightly but be ready to tighten your grip if necessary.

- Keep both hands on the wheel while you are driving unless you need to operate a control.

This standard hold enables you to turn the wheel immediately in either direction and is a feature of most safe and efficient steering techniques.

Make changes in direction smoothly and gradually. Make small changes in direction by turning the steering wheel without altering your hand hold.

To make more positive turns, use the pull–push method described next.

# Pull–push

With the pull–push method neither hand passes the twelve o'clock position. Your hands remain level with each other on the steering wheel except when you move a hand up for the initial pull or when you make small alterations in position. One hand grips and makes the turn, the other slides round its side of the wheel ready to continue the turn. The advantage of pull–push is that it keeps both hands on the wheel and allows an immediate turn in either direction at any point during steering.

The explanation of the pull–push method given below is for a left-hand turn. For a right-hand turn follow the same method starting with the right hand at 12 o'clock.

Start the turn with a pull and not a push because it gives better control.

Slide the left hand up to a higher position on the wheel, but not past the twelve o'clock point. The starting point will depend on the sharpness of the bend or turn.

Pull the wheel down with the left hand.

As the left hand pulls down, slide the right hand down, allowing the rim to slide through the right hand fingers. Keep the right hand level with the left hand until it nears the bottom of the wheel.

When you steer do you start with a pull rather than a push? If in the past you have tended to start with a push, practise pulling first. Notice how it contributes to the smoothness and control of your steering.

If more turn to the left is necessary start pushing up with the right hand and at the same time slide the left hand up the wheel, keeping it level with the right.

Repeat these movements until you achieve sufficient turn.

Straighten the vehicle after the turn by feeding the wheel back through the hands with similar but opposite movements to those used for the turn. Don't let the wheel spin back on its own.

# Rotational steering

In exceptional circumstances, for example during skidding or during very slow or high speed manoeuvres, this technique may be an option.

Hold the wheel using the standard hold described on page 78. The quarter-to-three position allows the greatest degree of turn without having to reposition a hand.

Most alterations to direction (up to about 120 degrees of steering wheel turn) can be made by turning the wheel while keeping a light but fixed hand hold.

For more acute turns (requiring more than about 120 degrees of steering wheel turn) reposition your lower hand at 12 o'clock and continue smoothly pulling down the wheel.

If you can see that a turn is going to require more than 120 degrees of steering wheel turn, place your leading hand at the top of the wheel before starting the turn.

If even more turn is required, place your other hand near the top of the wheel to continue the turning motion.

Straighten the wheel by using a similar series of movements but in the opposite direction. Although the self-centring action of the wheel assists the return, you must keep it under control.

## Manoeuvring at slow speeds and in confined spaces

Manoeuvring in a confined space sometimes requires rapid movements of the steering wheel. The standard pull–push technique generally provides effective steering, but on occasions, especially when reversing, other hand holds may give better control. Avoid trying to turn the steering wheel while the vehicle is stationary. This damages the tyres and puts excessive strain on the steering linkages, particularly in vehicles with power assisted steering (PAS).

### Reversing hold

Hold the wheel near the top with your right hand and low down with your left hand. If you find this position difficult, or need to improve your view to the left, put your left arm on the back of your seat. Look in your mirrors and over your shoulders to get a clear view. If the seat belt restricts your movement, release it but don't forget to put it back on.

## Advice on reversing

Reversing can be difficult, especially in a confined area. The faster it is done the more difficult it is to control, so always reverse slowly. Before you reverse:

- scan the area for suitability and obstructions
- ensure you have an unobstructed view
- use your mirrors to help you whilst reversing but look all round, don't rely on mirrors alone

- wind down your door window to give you more all round awareness
- get someone to help you if possible.

While reversing:

- travel slowly and slip the clutch if necessary – in automatic vehicles you can check the speed by using the left foot on the brake
- as you steer, the front of your vehicle moves out and could strike nearby objects – remember to look forward
- check around you for hazards.

If your reversing lights fail, use your indicator lights or brakelights to light the area behind you when it is dark, but be careful not to mislead other road users.

## Key points

- Don't rest your elbows on the window frame or arm rests because this reduces steering control.
- Hold the wheel lightly but be ready to tighten your grip when you need maximum steering effort.
- Keep both hands on the wheel when cornering, braking or driving through deep surface water.
- On slippery roads steer as delicately as possible or you may skid.

Accurate steering requires good observation, anticipation and planning. If the brakes are applied sharply or if the speed is too high, steering cannot be precise.

Acceleration, using gears, braking and steering

# Review

## In this chapter we have looked at:

- the skilled use of controls for moving, stopping and manoeuvring your vehicle
- getting maximum safety from the tyre grip available
- how acceleration and braking affect vehicle balance
- the importance of matching engine speed to road speed when you change gear
- skilled use of the gears in a range of circumstances
- using your brakes
- thinking, braking and safe stopping distances
- steering for maximum safety and control.

## Check your understanding

How and why does acceleration affect your ability to steer?

How and why does braking affect your ability to steer?

Why do you need to be in the correct gear to accelerate?

What is the basic driving safety rule?

When, if at all, should you use your gears to brake?

What is the safest way to lose speed gently in slippery conditions?

What factors affect thinking distance and braking distance?

What is the simplest rule to keep a safe distance from the vehicle in front?

What are the key points to remember for effective steering?

If you have difficulty in answering any of these questions, look back over the relevant part of this chapter to refresh your memory.

# Chapter 5
# Maintaining vehicle stability

**Use this chapter to find out:**

- how to minimise the risk of skidding
- what causes a skid
- what active safety features do to help stability and what they can't do
- how to correct a skid manually in a vehicle not fitted with active safety features.

# Controlling your vehicle's stability

A vehicle's stability is reduced when you brake, accelerate or steer because these actions produce forces that alter the vehicle's weight distribution and balance, and reduce tyre grip. A vehicle may skid when one or more of the tyres loses normal grip on the road. This chapter gives advice on how to avoid skidding, and what to do if a skid develops.

New vehicles are fitted with a growing range of active safety features to increase vehicle stability. The principles of ABS, traction control and electronic stability control (ESC) – also known as electronic stabililty programme (ESP) – are briefly explained here. Although the principles of each feature are similar, there are significant differences between manufacturers in how their particular device is activated and how it behaves.

**It is vital that you refer to the manufacturer's handbook** to know how your vehicle's safety features work and when they may intervene.

You may on occasions drive an older vehicle not fitted with ABS or other active safety features. The final part of this chapter explains how to deal with a skid manually in a vehicle without these devices.

# Avoiding skidding

Avoiding a skid by driving safely within the limits of the road conditions is better than having to correct one. Research shows that it is not poor road or weather conditions that cause skids but the driver's response to them. Skidding is caused by excessive speed, coarse steering, harsh acceleration or excessive or sudden braking. The real cause of the skid is therefore the driver.

Aim to control your vehicle so that it does not skid. This becomes more difficult when road or weather conditions deteriorate, but you can minimise the risk by driving more slowly and using your skills of observation, anticipation and planning.

## How does a skid happen?

A vehicle skids when one tyre or more loses normal grip on the road, causing an involuntary movement of the vehicle. This happens when the grip of tyres on the road becomes less than the force or forces acting on the vehicle:

These forces act on your vehicle whenever you operate the controls – the brake, the accelerator, the clutch or the steering wheel. If you brake or accelerate while steering round a bend or corner, two forces are combined. There is only limited tyre grip available so if these forces become too powerful they break the grip of the tyres on the road. Look back now at the diagram on page 61 which shows how each of these forces affects the vehicle's stability and reduces tyre grip.

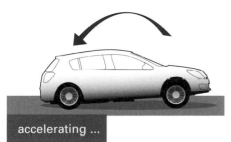

Braking, ...

*Never drive to the limits of the tyre grip available – always leave a safety margin to allow for the unforeseen.*

accelerating ...

*It takes much less force to break the grip of the tyres on a slippery road surface.*

and **cornering** are the forces that cause a vehicle to lose tyre grip.

# Reducing the risk of skidding

## Check your vehicle

The condition of your vehicle can reduce or increase the risk of skidding:

- **check tyre treads and tyre pressure regularly**
- **check the vehicle's brakes before you drive – defective brakes are especially dangerous on slippery surfaces.**

Avoid skidding in the first place – use observation, anticipation and planning to adjust your driving when the road surface may be slippery.

See Know your vehicle, page 164

## Observe – weather and road conditions to watch for

Skidding is more likely in bad weather conditions and on slippery road surfaces. Watch out for:

- snow, ice, frost, heavy rain
- wet mud, damp leaves or oil, which can create sudden slippery patches on the road surface
- cold spots in shaded areas, under trees, on slopes or hills – watch how other vehicles behave in icy weather
- dry loose dust or gravel
- a shower or rain after a long dry spell – accumulated rubber dust and oil mixed with water can create a very slippery surface
- worn road surfaces that have become polished smooth

- concrete – may hold surface water and become slippery, especially in freezing conditions
- cobbled roads – these become very slippery when wet
- changes in the road surface on bridges, which may be more slippery than the surrounding roads.

You are at greater risk from these hazards at corners and junctions because you are more likely to combine braking, accelerating and steering in these situations.

## Anticipate and plan – adjust your driving to the road conditions

Use your observation skills – watch out for and assess poor weather and road conditions accurately and adjust your speed accordingly:

- leave plenty of room for manoeuvre, reduce your speed and increase the distance you allow for stopping to match the road conditions – on a slippery surface a vehicle can take many times the normal distance to stop
- use lower revs in slippery conditions to avoid wheel spin, especially when moving off. Use a higher gear when travelling at low speeds
- on a slippery surface aim to brake, steer and change gear as smoothly as possible, so that you don't break the tyre grip
- use the principles of cornering (see Chapter 8) to negotiate corners carefully in slippery conditions.

# Recognising the cause of a skid

If your vehicle loses stability and a skid begins to develop, you need to recognise the cause of the skid. The commonest causes of skidding are:

- driving too fast for the circumstances
- harsh acceleration
- excessive or sudden braking
- coarse steering.

Speed in itself does not cause skidding as a constant speed exerts no change in the vehicle's balance; but at higher speeds, braking or turning places a much higher demand on tyre grip.

*Each skid is unique and every vehicle responds differently. How you apply the principles and techniques outlined in this chapter will depend entirely on the circumstances and on the vehicle you are driving.*

You need to be able to recognise different types of skid in the early stages so that you can respond appropriately and regain tyre grip as soon as possible.

## *Cause:* **Driving too fast for the circumstances**

At higher speeds you need more tyre grip to corner or stop. When surface grip is low, altering speed or direction can exceed the available grip, causing a skid. The faster you go the more likely this becomes. The vehicle's own weight or a change in road surface can reduce the grip of front or back tyres. Weight in the boot will alter the vehicle's normal balance and tyre grip.

## *Cause:* **Harsh acceleration**

Harsh acceleration can cause the wheels to spin, even at low speeds.

## *Cause:* **Excessive or sudden braking**

Excessive braking for the road conditions causes skidding because the tyres lose their grip.

## *Cause:* **Coarse steering**

A moving vehicle uses least tyre grip when travelling in a straight line. As soon as you start to corner you place extra demands on the tyre grip. If you steer too sharply for the speed you will cause the vehicle to understeer or oversteer. This may break the tyre grip and the vehicle will then go into a skid. Aim to make your steering as smooth as possible.

In different vehicles, you may need to negotiate the same corner at different speeds.

## **Understeer and oversteer**

Understeer is the tendency of a vehicle to turn less, and oversteer is the tendency of a vehicle to turn more in response to a given turn of the steering wheel. This can happen even at low speeds.

The tendency to understeer or oversteer is a characteristic of the vehicle itself coupled with the driver using excess speed for the circumstances. Historically, front wheel drive vehicles tended to understeer and rear wheel drive vehicles tended to oversteer. New vehicles may be designed to compensate for this tendency so take time to get to know the handling characteristics of a vehicle you are not familiar with.

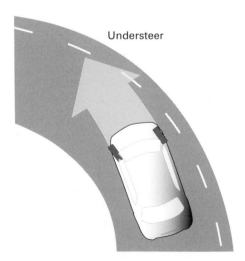

Understeer

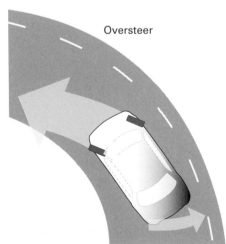

Oversteer

# How active safety features work

Activating a safety device means you are losing control of the vehicle – safety devices are not a replacement for *Roadcraft* skills.

Manufacturers are constantly seeking to improve vehicle stability with active safety features that can help safety and stability during braking, acceleration or steering. The active safety devices explained below are:

- antilock braking systems (ABS)
- traction control systems (TCS)
- and electronic stability control systems (ESC).

If an active safety system is fitted, you will see an icon light up on the dashboard when you turn on the ignition or start the engine. If more than one device is fitted, they may be displayed separately or combined in a single warning light.

*Vehicles fitted with active safety devices behave differently from vehicles without.*

These systems intervene at different points and some models have a deliberately delayed point of intervention. You must know how to use each device correctly in each vehicle that you drive. If you activate any of these active safety systems, you are not driving within the safe limits of the vehicle or the road conditions.

## Antilock braking systems (ABS)

Most modern vehicles are fitted with ABS, an electronic active safety device which adds to the conventional hydraulic braking system by giving you some ability to steer during harsh or emergency braking.

The footbrake applies the brakes to all four wheels at once, but ABS is designed to control the braking applied to individual wheels. It works by sensing when a wheel is slowing down and about to lockup. When this happens, ABS releases the brake on that wheel before it locks up fully. It reapplies the brakes once the wheel starts to rotate again.

The advantage of ABS is that it allows you to steer the vehicle under full braking power, because it prevents the wheels locking up.

Once ABS is activated, the driver has to maintain maximum pressure on the brake pedal throughout. ABS may reduce or lengthen the stopping distance of the vehicle compared with conventional brakes on different road surfaces but allows the driver to retain some steering control.

*ABS cannot increase the grip of the tyres on the road, nor can it fully prevent the possibility of the vehicle skidding.*

When ABS is activated you will see a warning light on the dashboard and will feel the brake pedal vibrate or judder momentarily as the system modulates the brake line pressures. If you become aware that the ABS is cutting in, you should learn from this and reduce your speed for the rest of the journey.

## Traction control systems (TCS)

When you accelerate, it is possible for the wheel turning power of the engine to exceed the amount of available tyre grip, especially when moving off on icy or slippery roads, on a steep hill or accelerating out of a corner. This may cause the driven wheels to spin. Wheel spin reduces both the vehicle's ability to accelerate and its stability.

Traction control systems work by controlling excess wheel spin on individual wheels. They apply independent braking to the spinning wheel. Some may also limit the wheel turning power of the engine to increase tyre grip.

TCS allows you to make maximum use of tyre grip, especially on slippery surfaces or where the friction of the road surface is uneven (for example, where one wheel grips the normal surface and the other slips on ice or snow).

When TCS is activated, you will see a warning light on the dashboard. If when you pull away from a standstill traction control cuts in, reduce pressure on the accelerator to regain control of the steering.

## Electronic Stability Control (ESC)

Electronic Stability Control is an extension of conventional antilock braking (ABS) and traction control (TCS) systems. It is designed to help the vehicle's stability by detecting when the vehicle is driven beyond its physical capabilities.

There is more variation between types of ESC than between types of ABS or TCS, so **it is vital to consult your vehicle handbook** and follow the manufacturer's advice on what to do if a skid develops.

Sensors working at each wheel work in combination with a sensor that monitors the rotation of the vehicle – called a yaw sensor. If these detect that the driver is about to lose control, the system intervenes and applies the brakes to individual wheels in order to correct understeer or oversteer and realign the vehicle to the driver's intended path. The intended path is detected by a sensor on the steering assembly so it is crucial that you steer in the direction you want to go.

Not all ESC systems have steering sensors; some only have yaw sensors. Most systems interact with the engine management system, reducing or increasing the engine power to the driven wheels. Some also interact with the transmission system.

*If you drive a vehicle beyond its physical capabilities, Electronic Stability Control does not guarantee that the vehicle will remain stable and under control.*

## Key points

- If you brake too hard, ABS prevents the wheel from locking up.

- If you accelerate too harshly, traction control prevents the wheel from excessive spinning.

- If you steer too sharply, electronic stability control can help prevent the resulting oversteer or understeer from developing into a skid.

*Different types and makes of safety system vary widely in how they operate and intervene. Never rely on them – you should drive in such a way that they are not necessary.*

# Skid control in vehicles fitted with active safety features

Skid control in a vehicle fitted with one or more of these active safety systems will depend on the features fitted.

If you regularly drive different vehicles, be aware that different manufacturers use a range of systems which intervene in different ways. **You must take note of the manufacturer's advice, and guidance in the driver's vehicle handbook**, so that you fully understand how each vehicle is likely to behave in extreme circumstances.

## Attitudes to vehicle safety technology

Some research suggests that ABS and other active safety devices may give some drivers a false sense of security, causing them to take more risks than they would in a vehicle without the safety features.

Safety features cannot change the laws of physics – they don't make a vehicle perform better or increase a driver's skill. They can help a driver who is on the point of losing control of the vehicle to regain control, provided the driver understands the specific feature and knows how to use it correctly.

# Correcting a skid in a vehicle without active safety features

There are still some fleet vehicles that are not fitted with any of the active safety features discussed in this chapter. If the vehicle you drive is one of these, the action you take to correct a skid will depend on whether the skid is a rear wheel, front wheel or four wheel skid. You may need to use rotational steering rather than pull–push to correct the direction of your vehicle.

## Correcting a rear wheel skid

In a rear wheel skid you feel the back of the vehicle swing out – on a corner or bend the swing is always initially to the outside of the curve.

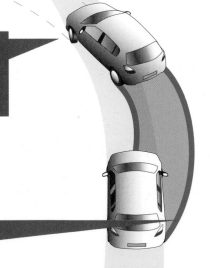

**3.** Gently steer the car back on to course. Do not overreact or the vehicle may skid in the opposite direction, especially if it has a rear wheel drive.

**4.** When it is safe to do so, gently apply power.

**2.** Steer in the direction of the skid until the rear of the vehicle stops sliding and the tyres regain their grip.

**1.** As soon as you feel the back of the car swing out, remove the cause of the skid:

release the accelerator

or

declutch and release the accelerator.

# Correcting a front wheel skid

In a front wheel skid you feel the front of the vehicle carry straight on when you are expecting it to steer left or right.

**2.** The natural reaction is to continue to steer vigorously to try to regain the original course

BUT if circumstances permit, steer in the direction of the skid to allow the tyres to regain grip. Once this happens, steer the vehicle back on to course.

**3.** Once back on course, apply power gently.

**1.** As soon as you feel the vehicle starting to understeer, remove the cause:

release the accelerator
or
declutch and release the accelerator

Roadcraft

## Correcting a four wheel skid

In a four wheel skid – usually the result of excessive or sudden braking causing all four wheels to lose grip on the road – you feel a lightness and loss of direction as all four wheels lock up and the vehicle begins to slide.

**2.** Release the accelerator or
declutch and release the accelerator, allowing the wheels to rotate and the tyres to regain their grip. At the same time steer in the direction you want the vehicle to go.

**3.** When it is safe to do so, gently apply power.

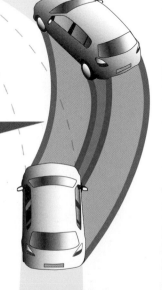

**1.** Remove the cause: release the brake.

# What to do in different circumstances

Once you have removed the initial cause of the skid, your next action may depend on the exact circumstances.

For instance:

**Do you need to steer in order to avoid a collision?**

      **YES  NO** ⟶ Maintain pressure on the brake.

**Is the road surface slippery?**

      **YES  NO** ⟶ On a non-slippery surface, release the brakes (except with **ABS**) sufficiently to allow the wheels to turn and restore steering control.

On a slippery surface you may need to pump the brakes rhythmically while steering to avoid a collision (cadence braking – see over page).

## Vehicles with different drives

Front, rear and four wheel drive vehicles each behave and respond differently in a skid. The method for correcting a skid is broadly the same for each type of vehicle, but understanding the characteristics of different types of drive can help you anticipate and respond to the vehicle's behaviour more effectively. Refer to your manufacturer's handbook for guidance.

**Do you know what type of drive your vehicle has?**

Get into the habit of checking the type of drive whenever you get into a new vehicle.

## Cadence braking (rhythm braking, pumping the brakes)

If you brake hard in wet or slippery conditions it is likely that your wheels will lock and you will lose steering control. Your vehicle will skid in a straight line and you may well collide with something before the skid ends.

Cadence braking (explained in Chapter 4) gives you a combination of braking and steering effect – braking while the brakes are on, steering while they are off. Pump the brakes with a deliberate movement, pausing momentarily when the brake pedal is fully depressed – but don't bounce the foot on and off the pedal.

See Chapter 4, *Acceleration etc.*, page 76, Cadence braking.

Brakes off –
steering regained

Cadence braking:

Brakes on –
no steering

# Aquaplaning

Aquaplaning occurs where a wedge of water builds up between the front tyres and the road surface, often because of thin or worn tyre tread. Whether you brake or steer, the vehicle will not respond. The safest solution is to remove pressure from the accelerator allowing the vehicle to lose speed and the tyres to regain their grip. Do not turn the steering wheel while aquaplaning because the vehicle will lurch whichever way the wheels are pointing when the tyres regain grip.

Build-up of standing water on the road surface causes aquaplaning

# Review

## In this chapter we have looked at:

- the forces affecting a vehicle's tyre grip
- how a driver's actions can cause a skid
- reducing the risk of skidding by observing, anticipating, and planning – and by regular vehicle maintenance
- how to recognise the cause of a skid
- how active safety systems work – antilock braking, traction control and electronic stability control
- how to correct a skid in a vehicle not fitted with active safety devices
- front wheel, rear wheel or four wheel skids
- cadence braking in older vehicles without ABS
- how to deal with aquaplaning.

## Check your understanding

What are the main causes of skidding?

What is meant by understeer and oversteer?

Can active safety systems enhance a vehicle's capabilities?

Explain briefly how ABS, traction control and ESC work.

What are the limitations of active safety systems?

How would you manually correct a front wheel skid?

What is cadence braking and when would you use this manual technique?

What is aquaplaning? What is the safest way to deal manually with this type of skid?

If you have difficulty in answering any of these questions, look back over the relevant part of this chapter to refresh your memory.

# Chapter 6
# Driver's signals

**Use this chapter to find out about:**

- the purpose of signals
- the range of signals available to you and when you should use them
- how to avoid confusion in giving and interpreting signals
- when to use arm signals
- why courtesy signals help road safety and positive driving attitudes
- how to assess and improve your skill at using signals.

# Developing your skill at using signals

Using signals may seem to be a basic skill, but many drivers don't use the full range of available signals consistently or to best effect. This chapter will help you improve your skill at using signals.

Giving information to other road users is a key part of information processing in the system of car control.

See Chapter 3, *The system of car control*, page 50, Information.

## The purpose of signals

Signals inform other road users of your presence or intentions. Think before you signal; indiscriminate signalling is not helpful to anyone.

> *Give a signal whenever it could benefit other road users.*

Whatever the situation, give signals clearly and in good time. Always make sure the meaning of your signal is clear. Sometimes a signal is not in itself enough to make your intentions clear and other road users may use your position and speed to interpret what your signals mean. When negotiating a roundabout, for example, your signals can be misinterpreted if you have not taken up the correct position for your intended exit.

## Key points

- Consider the need to give a signal on the approach to every hazard, and before you change direction or speed.
- Give a signal whenever it could benefit other road users.
- Remember that signalling does not give you any special right to carry out the actions you indicate.
- Follow the *Highway Code* – check your mirrors before you signal or manoeuvre.

## Avoid confusion

You also need to be cautious about how you interpret the signals of other road users. For example, does a vehicle flashing the left-hand indicator mean that the driver intends to:

- park the vehicle, possibly immediately after a left-hand junction?
- turn into a left-hand junction?
- carry straight on, having forgotten to cancel the last signal?

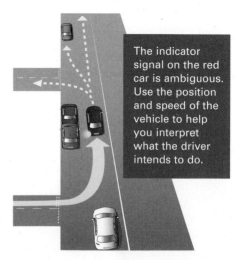

The indicator signal on the red car is ambiguous. Use the position and speed of the vehicle to help you interpret what the driver intends to do.

# The range of signals

The signals available to you are:
- indicators
- hazard warning lights
- brakelights
- headlights
- position of your vehicle
- horn signals
- arm signals
- courtesy signals (for example, raising a hand to thank another driver).

Select the most effective signal for the job. Any signal must be given in plenty of time if it is to benefit other road users. Be aware that when you change the speed or position of your vehicle you are also giving information to other road users.

## Using the indicators

The system of car control advises you to give a signal when another road user could benefit. This helps your driving because:
- it encourages you to be attentive and aware, especially of those behind you

- it reduces the number of hand movements you have to make
- it reduces signalling clutter

The purpose of signals is to warn other road users of your presence and/or your intention. Signals are informative and do not give right of way.

One signal should not cover two manoeuvres. Use your position to make your intentions clear to other road users.

## Cancelling indicator signals

Never take an indicator signal as proof of another driver's intention when you are waiting to emerge from a side turning. Look for supporting evidence such as an obvious slowing down or wheels turning before you move out.

Indicator mechanisms don't always self-cancel, especially when a turn is followed by a bend in the same direction. Take care to cancel the indicator yourself in such situations.

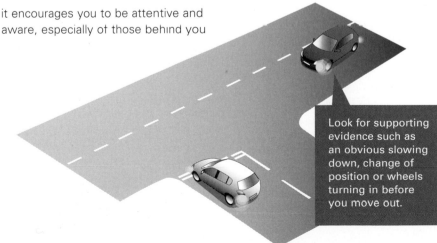

Look for supporting evidence such as an obvious slowing down, change of position or wheels turning in before you move out.

**Do you give clear signals to other road users?**

- Do you always signal when another road user could benefit?
- Do you signal your intentions clearly and in good time?
- Where possible do you choose a position that helps to make your intentions clear to other road users?

# Using hazard warning lights

Consider using hazard lights to alert other drivers to your presence when you have stopped. Don't use hazard lights when moving except on unrestricted multi-lane carriageways and motorways. Here you can use hazard lights briefly to warn the vehicles behind you that there is a hold-up ahead.

# Using brakelights

Brakelights are used to indicate either slowing down or your intention to stop. Always check your mirrors before using your brakes unless you are doing an emergency stop.

- Start braking well in advance of an anticipated hazard to alert the driver behind that you mean to slow down or stop, especially if the vehicle behind is too close. Avoid 'dabbing' the brakes: if your brakelights flash on and off but you don't slow down, you will confuse the drivers behind you.

- Remember that rear foglights are brighter than brakelights and may mask them when you are slowing down.

# Flashing your headlights

Flash your headlights when the horn would not be heard, and in place of the horn at night. Flashing your headlights should only be used for one purpose: to inform other road users that you are there. Never assume that another driver flashing their headlights is a signal to proceed.

Use a headlight flash in daylight:

- when speed makes it likely that the horn would not be heard, for example on a motorway or when signalling to a lorry driver in an enclosed cab
- to alert other drivers to your presence when you are approaching from behind, for example where a driver in the nearside lane of a motorway starts to pull out in front of you.

Use your judgement to decide the duration of the flash and how far in advance you should give it. This is critical and will depend on your speed. The purpose of flashing your headlights is solely to inform the other driver of your presence. It does not give you the right to overtake regardless of the circumstances.

During darkness flash your headlights to inform other road users of your presence:

- on the approach to a hill crest or narrow hump back bridge
- when travelling along narrow winding roads

- before overtaking another vehicle – flash your headlights early enough to enable the driver of the other vehicle to react to them.

Don't flash your headlights when they might be misunderstood by road users for whom they are not intended.

## Using the horn

Only use the horn when it is necessary to warn other road users of your presence. If you see that another road user is not aware of your presence, first choose an appropriate position and speed so that you can stop safely.

Consider using the horn on the approach to hazards where the view is very limited, such as a blind summit or bridge on a single track road. Never use the horn to challenge or rebuke other road users.

Driver's signals

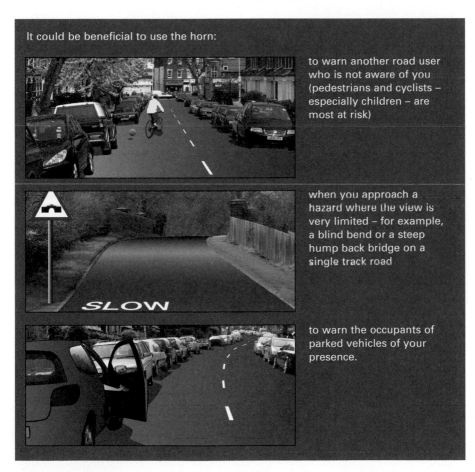

It could be beneficial to use the horn:

to warn another road user who is not aware of you (pedestrians and cyclists – especially children – are most at risk)

when you approach a hazard where the view is very limited – for example, a blind bend or a steep hump back bridge on a single track road

to warn the occupants of parked vehicles of your presence.

## Using arm signals

Although arm signals are no longer in regular use, you should know what they mean and how to give them according to the *Highway Code*. Be aware that many young drivers are less familiar with arm signals and may not understand them.

Think about using arm signals to reinforce other signals in ambiguous situations.

Do not use arm signals when you need both hands on the steering wheel to control the car, such as during braking or cornering.

Arm signals might be useful:

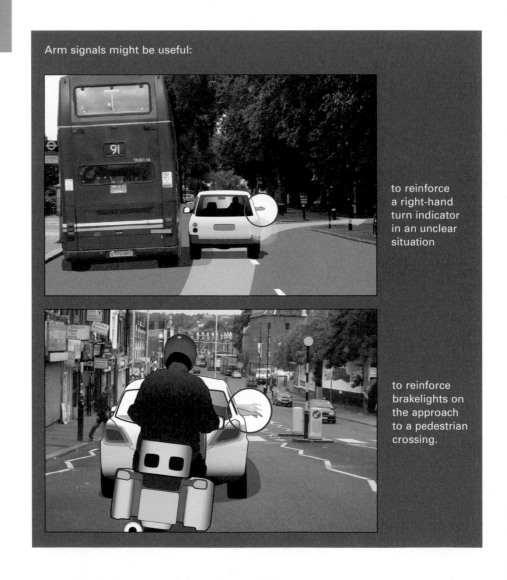

to reinforce a right-hand turn indicator in an unclear situation

to reinforce brakelights on the approach to a pedestrian crossing.

## Using courtesy signals

Courtesy signals encourage cooperative use of the road space and help to increase road safety. Acknowledging the courtesy of other road users encourages good driving and helps foster positive attitudes. Using a courtesy signal to defuse a potential conflict can make a real difference to road safety. Use courtesy signals:

- to thank another driver for letting you go first

- to apologise when you have unintentionally caused inconvenience to another road user.

Use either hand to give a courtesy signal but not at the risk of your steering control. You can signal without removing your hand from the wheel by raising your palm or nodding your head. Or you can ask your passenger to signal for you. But make sure that your courtesy signal cannot be mistaken for a 'waving on' signal.

**On your route home from work, make a conscious effort to give and acknowledge courtesy signals.**

- How does this affect your own state of mind?

- How does it influence the actions of other drivers?

- Do you think you tend to give courtesy signals more or less often than other drivers?

Ask other people who know your driving whether they agree with your self assessment.

## Responding to other people's signals

Signals other than those given by authorised officials should be treated with caution. If someone beckons you to move forward, always check for yourself whether it is safe to do so.

If someone beckons you to move forward, always check for yourself whether it is safe to do so.

Roadcraft

# Review

**In this chapter we have looked at:**

- the place of signals in the system of car control
- why it is important to give signals clearly
- the different signals available to you, and how and when to use them
- how courtesy signals can help road safety.

## Check your understanding

List the full range of signals that you can use to give information to other road users.

When should you consider signalling?

What should you do before you signal or manoeuvre?

Why must you take care in interpreting the signals of other road users?

Why should you only signal when someone else could benefit?

Why do left-hand junctions pose problems for interpreting indicator signals?

In what circumstances should hazard warning lights be used?

When and for what purpose should you flash your headlights?

When should you use the horn?

How do courtesy signals contribute to road safety and positive driving attitudes?

If you have difficulty in answering any of these questions, look back over the relevant part of this chapter to refresh your memory.

# Chapter 7
# Positioning

**Use this chapter to find out about:**

- how to position your vehicle on the road for safety
- which hazards to look for on the nearside of the road
- how to improve your nearside view
- what is the best position for following another vehicle
- how to position your vehicle for bends and corners.

# Developing skill at positioning your vehicle

For advice on positioning on the motorway, see Chapter 10, *Driving on motorways and multi-lane carriageways.*

Positioning is a crucial element in the system of car control.

See Chapter 3, *The system of car control*, page 51.

The ideal road position depends on many things: safety, observation, traffic conditions, road layout, cornering, manoeuvrability, assisting traffic flow and making your intentions clear. Always consider safety before anything else, and never sacrifice safety for any other advantage.

*Put the car in the best position for you to see, with due regard to safety.*

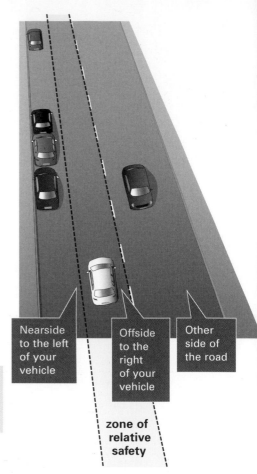

Nearside to the left of your vehicle

Offside to the right of your vehicle

Other side of the road

zone of relative safety

## Safety position on the approach to hazards

By carefully choosing your position you can reduce the risk of having a collision. Be aware of hazards on both sides of your vehicle. To the nearside there is a risk of coming into conflict with cyclists and pedestrians (especially children), and parked vehicles and their occupants. You also need to be aware of other vehicles pulling out from junctions. To the offside, there is a risk of coming into conflict with oncoming vehicles in the centre of the road.

Between the two extremes is a zone that is *relatively* free of hazards, but always adapt your position and speed to the actual circumstances.

The system of car control provides a safe and methodical approach to hazards. Dangers can come from anywhere but you will generally have less time to react to hazards coming from the nearside. On narrow roads and in one-way systems you need to pay equal attention to both sides of the road.

## Roadside hazards

Common roadside hazards to look out for are:

- pedestrians, especially children, stepping off the footpath
- parked vehicles and their occupants
- cyclists, especially children
- horses
- joggers – where there is no footpath
- concealed junctions
- spray from kerbside puddles.

If you identify hazards on the nearside, take a position closer to the crown of the road. This has two benefits:

- it gives you a better view
- it provides more space in which to take avoiding action if you need to.

If oncoming traffic makes it unsafe to take this position, or if the road is too narrow, reduce your speed. There is an important trade-off between your speed and the clearance around your vehicle. The less space you have, the slower you should go. Be prepared to stop if necessary.

Keep as far from rows of parked vehicles as circumstances allow. A good rule of thumb is to leave at least enough space for an opening door to the side of any parked vehicles. If you can't move out, slow down. Get into the habit of asking yourself *'Could I stop in time if a child ran out?'* One in three children hit by cars does not look first.

The less space you have the slower you should go

If traffic conditions allow, take a position closer to the crown of the road.

## Improving the view into nearside road junctions

Position yourself so that you can see as much of the road ahead as possible and so that other road users can see you. You can improve your view into nearside roads by positioning your vehicle towards the crown of the road. This also makes you more visible to vehicles pulling out from nearside junctions. But you must take into account any vehicles on the other side of the road. Take a position that minimises the overall danger from both sides of the road.

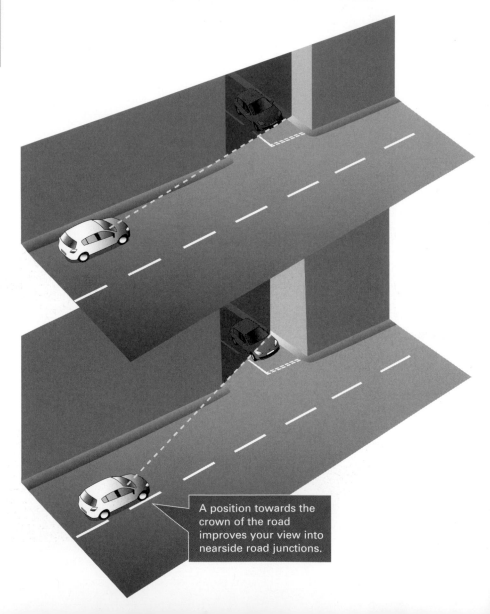

A position towards the crown of the road improves your view into nearside road junctions.

## Following position

In a stream of traffic, always keep a safe distance behind the vehicle in front. Follow the two-second rule. Leave a gap of *at least* two seconds between you and the vehicle front, depending on conditions.

See Chapter 4, *Acceleration, using gears, braking and steering*, page 75, The two-second rule.

Keeping your distance increases your safety because:

- you have a good view, and can increase it along both sides by slight changes of position – this enables you to be fully aware of what is happening on the road ahead
- you can stop your vehicle safely if the driver in front brakes firmly without warning
- you can extend your braking distance so that the driver behind has more time to react
- you can see when it is safe to move into the overtaking position
- you suffer less from the effects of spray from the vehicle in front.

Positioning

The driver is too close to the vehicle in front and cannot see the hazards in the shaded area.

The driver is keeping a good safe position and can see all the hazards. The driver could see even more by moving slightly to the nearside or offside.

## Overtaking position

See Chapter 9, *Overtaking*, page 135.

If you intend to overtake, position your vehicle to get the best possible view and opportunity by moving into the overtaking position. This is generally closer to the vehicle in front than the following position and you should only use it in readiness for overtaking. If a hazard (e.g. an oncoming vehicle, a road junction) comes into view, move back to an appropriate following distance from the vehicle in front.

As you move closer to the vehicle in front the driver is likely to realise that you want to overtake. Be careful not to intimidate the other driver or to appear aggressive by following too closely. This is dangerous and counter-productive. Following too closely can cause the other driver to speed up, making it more difficult to overtake.

## Position for turning

Your position for turning depends on the other traffic, the road width and layout, the position of any obstacles and the effect of these obstacles on traffic behaviour. Generally the best

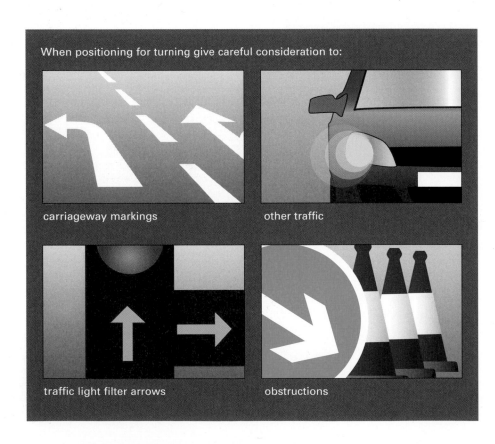

When positioning for turning give careful consideration to:

carriageway markings

other traffic

traffic light filter arrows

obstructions

position on the approach to a junction is on the nearside of the road for a left turn and towards the centre line for a right turn.

If you intend to turn right and oncoming traffic is encroaching on your side of the road, move back in from the centre line.

If you intend to turn left and the corner has a sharp angle, is obscured, or pedestrians are present, approach the corner from further out than normal. Move further out in good time. Avoid 'swan necking' – approaching close to the nearside and then swinging out to the right just before turning into the junction.

Positioning

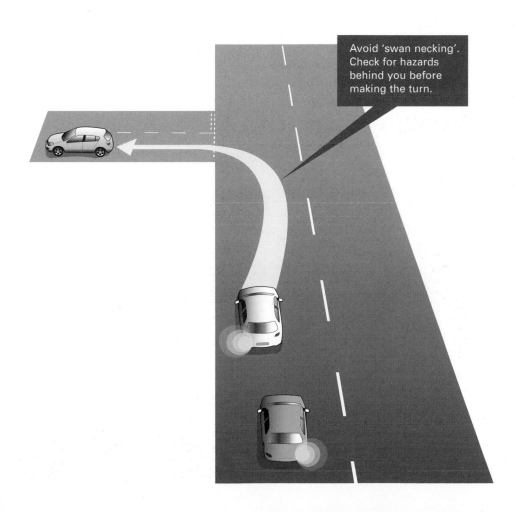

Avoid 'swan necking'. Check for hazards behind you before making the turn.

## Positioning at crossroads

The *Highway Code* advises that two
vehicles turning across each other at
a crossroads should pass offside to
offside; but where traffic conditions,
the junction layout or the position of the
other vehicle makes this impractical,
you should pass nearside to nearside.
Take extra care on a nearside to
nearside pass because your view of
the road is blocked by the other
vehicle. Look carefully
for oncoming traffic.

Passing offside to offside

Passing nearside to nearside

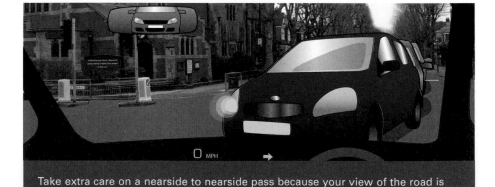

Take extra care on a nearside to nearside pass because your view of the road is
obstructed by the other vehicle.

## Position for stopping behind other vehicles

Before you come to a stop think about your next move. Position your vehicle so that you can continue with minimum inconvenience to yourself and other road users.

Stopping well short of the vehicle in front gives you several advantages:

- you maintain a good view of the road

- you are able to move around the vehicle ahead if it stalls or suffers a breakdown

- if you are hit from behind, the vehicle ahead is less likely to be affected

- the space in front of you is a safe haven for a bike or motorcycle

- if you become aware that a vehicle approaching behind has left braking too late, you can move forward to allow it extra space to stop in

- facing uphill, if the vehicle ahead starts to roll back towards you, you have time to warn the driver

An example of using your stopping position to increase safety is where there are traffic lights at roadworks close to a bend. Consider stopping before or on the approach to the bend so that drivers who come up behind can see you.

## Parking

Park your vehicle safely: do not leave it where it can cause inconvenience or danger to others. If you park on a hill, put the vehicle in a low gear and consider turning your wheels into the kerb.

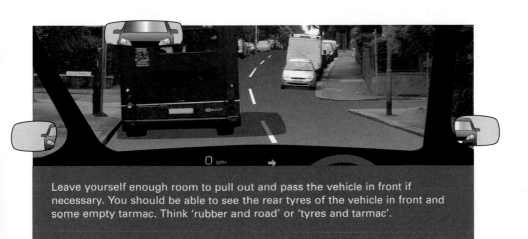

Leave yourself enough room to pull out and pass the vehicle in front if necessary. You should be able to see the rear tyres of the vehicle in front and some empty tarmac. Think 'rubber and road' or 'tyres and tarmac'.

# Review

**In this chapter we have looked at:**

- the factors to consider when choosing a road position
- why a position towards the centre of the road is *relatively* risk free
- some common roadside hazards
- where to position your vehicle if nearside hazards are present
- where to position your vehicle for following and overtaking a vehicle in front
- how to position your vehicle for turning and stopping
- how to turn past another vehicle at a crossroads.

**Check your understanding**

What is the most important factor in choosing your road position?

List some common nearside hazards that you should take into account when deciding on your position. What hazards should you look out for on the other side of the road?

If you drive down a road where the space to the sides is restricted, what should you do?

How much clearance should you generally give parked vehicles?

How can you improve your view into nearside junctions?

What are the advantages of keeping your distance from the vehicle in front?

How should you approach a left-hand junction when pedestrians are present?

Why do you need to be careful if you pass nearside to nearside at a junction?

If you have difficulty in answering any of these questions, look back over the relevant part of this chapter to refresh your memory.

# Chapter 8
# Cornering

**Use this chapter to find out about:**

- the principles of cornering
- the forces involved in cornering
- the factors which affect your vehicle's ability to corner
- how to use the limit point to judge your speed for a corner
- how to use the system of car control for cornering
- the best position to adopt as you drive round a bend.

# Developing your skill at cornering

Cornering – driving a car round a corner, curve or bend – is one of the main driving activities, and it is important to get it right. When you corner, your vehicle loses stability and you place extra demands on the tyre grip available. The faster you go and the tighter the bend, the greater these demands are.

This chapter explains how to apply the system of car control to cornering, starting with some general principles and then going on to look at the forces involved in cornering, the factors affecting your vehicle's ability to corner safely, and how to use the system of car control in conjunction with limit point analysis to corner safely.

See Chapter 3 *The system of car control*, page 50.

> *Over half of all fatal accidents for drivers under 30 are the result of the driver losing control on a bend or a curve.*

# Using the system to corner safely

Cornering is potentially dangerous so you should use the system of car control to help you carry out the manoeuvre safely. Each phase of the system is relevant but processing information is especially important. Correctly assessing the severity of the bend is essential for safety.

## Four key principles for safe cornering

- Your vehicle should be in the correct position on the approach.

- You should be travelling at the correct speed for the corner or bend.

- You should have the correct gear for that speed.

- You should be able to stop safely within the distance you can see to be clear.

Applying these principles to the variations in bend, visibility, traffic conditions, road surface conditions, and other factors calls for good judgement and planning. Before looking in more detail at using the system of car control for cornering, think about the factors that affect a vehicle's ability to corner safely.

# Cornering forces

A moving vehicle is most stable when its weight is evenly distributed, its engine is just pulling without increasing road speed, and it is travelling in a straight line. It will continue to travel in a straight line unless you apply some other force to alter its direction. When you steer, the turning force to alter direction comes from the action of the front tyres on the road. You saw in Chapter 4 that this force depends on tyre grip. If the front tyre grip is broken, the car will continue in a straight line. On tighter bends, at higher speeds and in heavier vehicles, the demands on tyre grip are greater.

Three forces reduce tyre grip:
- **steering**
- **accelerating**
- **braking**.

The more you brake or accelerate the less tyre grip you have for steering.

The faster you go into a corner or bend, the more tyre grip you need to keep your position.

If one or more of these forces causes loss of tyre grip, the vehicle will continue in a straight line rather than turning. So in a left-hand bend, as you lose tyre grip, your vehicle drifts to the right of your intended position and in a right-hand bend it drifts to the left. The design of the vehicle will reduce or increase this effect.

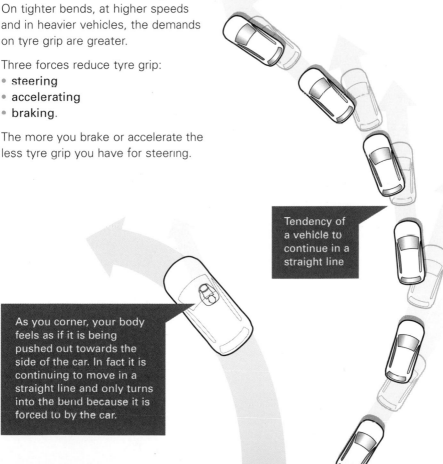

Tendency of a vehicle to continue in a straight line

As you corner, your body feels as if it is being pushed out towards the side of the car. In fact it is continuing to move in a straight line and only turns into the bend because it is forced to by the car.

# Vehicle characteristics

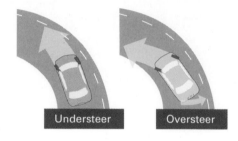

Understeer     Oversteer

## Roadworthiness

Vehicles vary in their ability to corner, and they only corner to the best of their ability if they are well maintained. Steering, suspension, shock absorbers, tyres, tyre pressures and the loading of the vehicle all affect its balance and tyre grip when cornering. Position loads evenly so they don't upset the balance of the vehicle.

*Make sure that your vehicle and tyres are in good condition and that you keep your tyre pressures at the recommended levels.*

## Vehicle specification

The specifications that affect the handling characteristics of a vehicle are:

- the type of drive – front wheel, rear wheel or four wheel
- suspension and damping
- traction control, if fitted
- adaptive suspension, if fitted
- the drive ratio and central differential characteristics on a four wheel drive vehicle
- dynamic stability control programmes.

## Understeer and oversteer

Understeer is the tendency of a vehicle to turn less, and oversteer is the tendency of a vehicle to turn more in response to a given turn of the steering wheel. The tendency to understeer or oversteer is a characteristic of the vehicle itself and depends mainly on what sort of drive the vehicle has. Most front wheel drive vehicles understeer and some rear wheel drive vehicles oversteer. However, some modern vehicles are designed to compensate for these tendencies. Make sure you know the different steering characteristics of each vehicle you drive and adapt your driving on corners and bends.

In a front wheel drive car, you will increase understeer if you:

- enter the bend too fast
- apply too much power in the bend
- steer too sharply.

You can reduce this understeer by reducing power and/or steering. But if you reduce power too much and too suddenly, you may convert the understeer to oversteer (known as 'lift-off oversteer').

A rear wheel drive car initially behaves in the same way, but if you apply too much power on a slippery surface any understeer may convert quite suddenly to oversteer. Correct the steering promptly in the opposite direction to the bend.

Four wheel drive cars provide better tyre grip all round but when driven to extremes they behave in a similar way to the front or rear wheel drive model from which they are derived.

## Camber and superelevation

Road surfaces usually slope to help drainage. The normal slope falls from the crown of the road to the edges and is called crown camber.

- **On a left-hand bend** camber increases the effect of your steering because the road slopes down in the direction of the turn.

- **On a right-hand bend** camber reduces the effect of steering because the road slopes away from the direction of the turn.

This applies if you keep to your own side of the road but if you cross over the crown to the other side of the road, the camber will have the opposite effect on your steering.

In many places, especially at junctions, the slope across the road surface can be at an unexpected angle. Whatever the slope, if it falls in the direction of your turn it will increase the effect of your steering but if it rises in the direction of your turn it will reduce the effect of your steering. Take this into account when deciding your position and speed for a bend.

Superelevation is where the whole width of the road is banked up towards the outside edge of the bend, making the slope favourable for cornering in both directions (similar to banking on a race track).

> **Observe how camber affects your steering**
>
> On your next journey, observe the camber whenever you corner. Notice how it affects the steering and balance of your vehicle. Pick out one or two sections of familiar road where cornering is tricky and work out whether unexpected camber is a factor.

## Summary of factors affecting cornering

The factors that determine your vehicle's ability to corner are:

- speed
- the amount of steering you apply
- the amount of acceleration and/or braking
- the characteristics of the vehicle
- the slope across the road surface – camber and superelevation
- the road surface and how the weather has affected its grip.

Crown camber

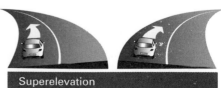

Superelevation

# The system of car control and the limit point

The system of car control helps you plan how to approach and negotiate corners and bends. Information processing and the four phases of the system – **position, speed, gear** and **acceleration** – are the key factors that you must consider when cornering.

As you approach a bend, seek as much information as possible about the severity of the bend using all the observational aids and clues available to you (weather, road surface, road signs, road markings, the line made by lamp posts and trees, the speed and position of oncoming traffic, the angle of headlights at night, etc.). The limit point gives you a systematic way of judging the correct speed to use through the bend.

Be aware of the foreshortening effect when you go uphill or downhill. The slope will make the limit point look nearer than it is so that it will take longer to reach.

## How to use the limit point to help you corner

The limit point is the furthest point to which you have an uninterrupted view of the road surface. On a level stretch of road, or on a right-hand bend, this is where the right-hand edge of the road appears to meet the left-hand edge in the distance. On a left-hand bend, the limit point is where the edge of the road meets the central white line (or the centre of the road if there is no white line). To drive safely you must be able to stop within the distance you can see to be clear – that is, the distance between you and the limit point. The more distant the limit point, the faster you can go because you have more space to stop in; the closer the limit point, the slower you must go because you have less space to stop in.

As you approach and go through a bend the limit point appears at first to be stationary, then to move away at a constant speed and finally to sprint away to the horizon as you come out of the bend. Watching the limit point enables you to match your speed to the speed at which this point appears to move. If it is moving away from you, you may accelerate. If it is coming closer to you or standing still, you must decelerate or brake. Even when the bend is not constant, you can still match your speed to the apparent movement of the limit point, because this will vary with the curvature of the bend. Acceleration sense is useful here.

Using the limit point together with the system helps you:

- adjust your speed so you can stop safely within the distance you can see to be clear
- decide the correct speed to approach and negotiate the bend
- assess the correct speed to go round the bend, selecting the correct gear for the bend
- decide the point at which to start accelerating.

Read the diagram from the bottom of the page upwards

### Coming out of the bend

As the bend starts to straighten out your view begins to open up, and the limit point ● starts to move away more quickly.

You can then accelerate steadily as you straighten your steering.

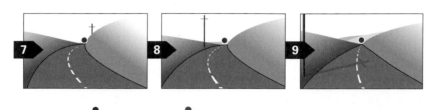

### Entering the bend

Just before you enter the bend the limit point ● begins to move round at a constant speed. Adjust your speed to the speed of this movement.

You now have the correct speed to go round the bend. Select the gear to match this speed before entering the bend.

### Approaching the bend

At first the limit point ● appears to stay at the same point in the road. Adjust your speed so you can stop safely within the remaining distance.

As you approach the bend take information about the sharpness of the bend and carefully assess the appropriate speed for cornering.

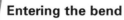

The limit point technique is self-adjusting – as road visibility and conditions deteriorate you need more distance in which to stop, and so you must reduce your speed to compensate.

Use the limit point *as well as* other observation links – get into the habit of looking across or beyond the bend as you approach it. You may spot a hazard just *after* the bend – for example a warning sign or a chevron marker indicating a further bend. In this case it would be inappropriate to use the limit point alone to set your speed.

Where a road is not wide enough for two vehicles to pass, consider doubling your stopping distance to give an oncoming vehicle enough space to stop as well. On a left hand bend on a single track road, the limit point is where the two kerb lines meet.

**Practise matching your speed to the movement of the limit point.**

Try this on different types of bend – from very gradual to hairpin – and note how using the limit point enables you to adjust to the characteristics of each bend. Always adjust your speed so that you can stop safely within the distance you can see to be clear.

Make a special point of using the limit point to set your speed for bends and corners on roads you know well. It is on familiar routes that your attention is most likely to wander.

# How to use the system for cornering

## Information

On the approach to a corner or bend you should be constantly scanning the road for information, especially about:

- traffic in front and behind
- the road surface and the effect of weather conditions on it
- the limit point.

Firstly, look across the bend through gaps in hedges or between buildings for more information. Use the curved line of hedgerows and lamp posts to give you information about the severity of the bend. Look for early warning of other hazards as well.

*Match your speed to the speed at which the limit point moves away from you, provided you can stop safely within the distance that you can see to be clear.*

## Position

You need to consider three things when positioning your vehicle for cornering:

- safety
- view
- stability.

### Safety

Position yourself so that you are least likely to come into conflict with other road users: for example, look out for pedestrians to your nearside and oncoming traffic to your offside. Never sacrifice safety for position.

## How you can get the best view

Your position will determine how much you can see when you enter a bend. Put the car in the best position for you to see, with due regard to safety. The position that gives you the clearest view is different for a left-hand bend and right-hand bend.

- *Right-hand bends* – position yourself towards the left of your road space, leaving enough clearance for parked vehicles and pedestrians. Watch out for blind junctions or exits, adverse camber and poor condition of the nearside road surface.

For right-hand bends, the nearside gives an earlier view into the bend.

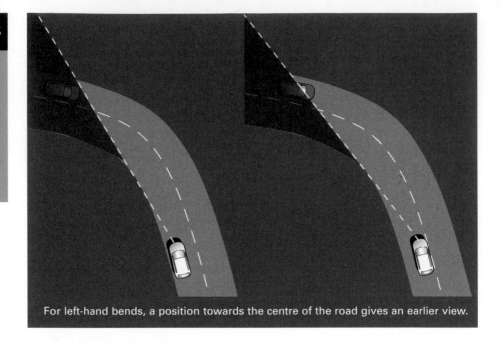

For left-hand bends, a position towards the centre of the road gives an earlier view.

- *Left-hand bends* – position yourself towards the centre line so that you get an early view round the bend. Before you take this position consider:
  - approaching traffic or other offside dangers which need a greater margin of safety
  - whether your position might mislead other traffic as to your intentions
  - whether or not you will gain any advantage at low speed or on an open bend.

## Speed

When you are in the correct position for the bend, use the limit point to judge the safe speed to drive round the bend. Where the bend is a constant curve, the limit point remains at a constant distance from you. Keep your speed constant. If the curve changes, reassess your speed and reapply the system.

To assess the correct speed for a bend, also consider:

- the severity of the bend
- the view into the bend
- your vehicle's characteristics
- road and road surface conditions
- traffic conditions
- weather conditions.

Remember your aim is to be able to stop safely within the distance you can see to be clear, not to take the bend as fast as possible.

## Gear

When you have achieved the correct speed and before you enter the bend, choose the appropriate gear for that speed. Select the gear that gives you greatest flexibility.

Think also how you expect to accelerate on the far side of the bend. If you expect to come out of the bend into a 30 mph area, plan for gentle acceleration. If the national speed limit applies to the other side of the bend, consider entering the bend in a gear that will provide maximum acceleration out of it. But always take into account the condition of the road surface: in wet or slippery conditions, if you accelerate harshly in a low gear you may cause wheel spin and lose steering control.

See Chapter 4, *Acceleration, using gears, braking and steering*, page 66, Using the gears.

## Acceleration

Where the bend is a constant curve, the limit point remains at a constant distance from you. Apply gentle pressure to the accelerator to maintain constant road speed through the curve until the limit point begins to move away. If the bend tightens, the limit point will appear to move closer, so reduce your speed accordingly to stay within a safe stopping distance.

If there are no hazards, start to accelerate when the limit point begins

to move away and you begin to straighten your steering.

As you continue to straighten your steering, increase acceleration to match the limit point. Accelerate until you reach the speed limit or the appropriate speed for the circumstances.

**Using the system of car control to corner**

- Do you position yourself to get the best possible view when cornering, with due regard to safety?

- Think about your driving behaviour on more open roads. As you plan your approach to corners, what's your priority?

- Do you think first about the correct speed and gear for control on the curve, or about safe stopping distance?

- Next time you take a significant corner on an open road, imagine there is a pregnant woman with a toddler in a pushchair about to cross the road just beyond your limit point. Does this alter your driving?

# Review

**In this chapter we have looked at:**

- the four principles of safe cornering
- the forces acting on a vehicle on bends and corners
- the characteristics that affect a vehicle's ability to corner
- how camber affects the ability to corner
- the use of the system of car control for cornering
- the technique of limit point analysis
- how to position yourself on the approach to a bend
- how to reduce the curvature of a bend
- how to assess the correct speed for a bend.

**Check your understanding**

What are the four principles of safe cornering?

What are the forces that reduce tyre grip when cornering?

Why are you less able to steer if you brake or accelerate sharply?

In which direction do you go if tyre grip is lost on a right-hand bend?

How does camber affect cornering?

What is meant by the limit point and how do you use it to corner safely?

Where would you position your vehicle when entering a right-hand bend and what hazards would you need to take into account?

If you have difficulty in answering any of these questions, look back over the relevant part of this chapter to refresh your memory.

# Chapter 9
# Overtaking

**Use this chapter to find out about:**

- how to overtake safely

- how to overtake moving vehicles

- which special hazards you need to consider before overtaking

- how to help other drivers to overtake you.

# Developing your skill at overtaking safely

Overtaking is hazardous because it may bring you into the path of other vehicles. It is a complex manoeuvre in which you need to consider the primary hazard of the vehicle(s) you want to overtake, as well as a number of secondary hazards as the primary hazard moves amongst them. It requires you to negotiate dynamic hazards (moving vehicles) as well as fixed ones (e.g. road layout).

This section describes the general principles of using the system of car control to do this manoeuvre safely. Training will further develop your ability to apply the system to dynamic hazards in practice.

## Key safety points

- Don't overtake where you cannot see far enough ahead to be sure it is safe.

- Avoid causing other vehicles (overtaken, following or oncoming) to alter position or speed.

- Before starting to overtake, always ensure you can move back to the nearside in plenty of time.

- Always be ready to abandon overtaking if a new hazard comes into view.

- Do not overtake in situations where you might come into conflict with other road users.

- When possible, avoid overtaking three abreast to leave yourself a margin of safety.

- Never overtake on the nearside on multi-lane carriageways except in slow-moving queues of traffic where offside queues are moving more slowly.

Overtaking is potentially dangerous and you need good judgement if it is to be safe. This comes with experience and practice but even experienced drivers need to be extremely cautious. Always be patient and leave a margin of safety to allow for errors.

*Remember that overtaking is your decision and you can reconsider it at any point. If in doubt, hold back.*

## Passing stationary vehicles

When passing stationary vehicles, use the system to approach and assess the hazard and to pass it with safety. Take account of the position and speed of oncoming traffic, the position and speed of following traffic and the presence of pedestrians or other roadside hazards, especially on the nearside (see Chapter 7). If the situation allows, leave at least a door's width when passing a stationary vehicle.

## Overtaking moving vehicles

Overtaking a moving vehicle is more complicated because the situation is changing all the time. You need to consider the speed and acceleration capabilities of your own vehicle, the physical features of the road and the relative speeds of other vehicles. You also need a good sense of where your own and other vehicles are in relation to gaps in the traffic.

# How to overtake

A vehicle to be overtaken is a moving hazard, so use the system of car control to deal with it safely. You need to observe and plan carefully, to judge speed and distance accurately, and to be alert to possible secondary hazards. Thoughtless overtaking is dangerous.

The following pages describe two overtaking situations:

- **where you are able to overtake immediately** (approaching, overtaking and returning to your own side of the road) in one continuous manoeuvre

- where other hazards require you to take up a following position before you can safely overtake.

In real life overtaking usually involves multiple hazards. Any overtaking situation can change rapidly and become complicated by further hazards (for example, new oncoming vehicles, or slower vehicles further ahead on your side of the road). In learning to negotiate these complex hazards, you may be required to consider and apply the system more than once in an overtaking manoeuvre. As you gain practice and confidence, you will learn to view the number of hazards as one complex picture, and to use fewer applications.

Although the same general rules apply when overtaking hazards other than a vehicle, always assess the specific circumstances. Speed or the sound of a horn can startle horses. Cyclists, especially children, can be erratic so allow them plenty of room. Give motorcycles plenty of room too; if you are too close, your slip stream could destabilise them.

*The following pages offer general advice but overtaking a moving vehicle involves complex, dynamic hazards. You need accurate observation, planning, information processing and judgement, and overtaking technique is best learned under guidance in a moving vehicle.*

Overtaking

# Where you are able to overtake immediately

Once you have checked that all the other conditions (e.g. clear view ahead, sufficient space, absence of oncoming traffic, safe return gap) are suitable for immediate overtaking, and there is no other factor which prevents you, work through the stages of the system to pass the slower vehicle(s) and return to your own side of the road. Use your mirrors and the appropriate signals throughout.

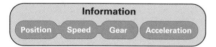

Information

Position | Speed | Gear | Acceleration

## Information

Observe the road ahead for other actual and potential dangers – physical features, position and movement of other people and weather/road conditions.

Identify:

- a safe stretch of road along which you have adequate vision

- what is happening behind

- a gap into which you can safely return

- the relative speed of your own vehicle and the vehicle(s) you intend to overtake.

Consider the need to give information to any other road users.

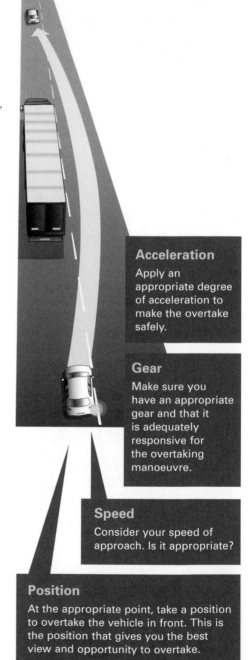

**Acceleration**
Apply an appropriate degree of acceleration to make the overtake safely.

**Gear**
Make sure you have an appropriate gear and that it is adequately responsive for the overtaking manoeuvre.

**Speed**
Consider your speed of approach. Is it appropriate?

**Position**
At the appropriate point, take a position to overtake the vehicle in front. This is the position that gives you the best view and opportunity to overtake.

# Where other hazards require you to follow before you can safely overtake

## Following position

Where you are gaining on a vehicle in front but can see it is not possible to overtake immediately, reduce your speed so that you can follow at a safe distance.

Observe and assess the road and traffic conditions ahead for an opportunity to overtake safely and when you see one, move into an overtaking position. Ask yourself the questions below.

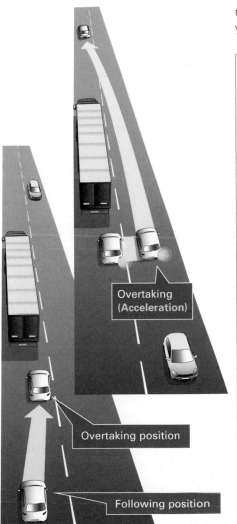

Overtaking (Acceleration)

Overtaking position

Following position

- Does the road layout present a hazard?
- What is the speed of the vehicle(s) to be overtaken?
- Is/are the driver(s) ahead likely to overtake?
- Have I taken into account the speed and performance of my own vehicle?
- What is the likely response of the driver and occupants of the vehicle in front?
- What is the speed of oncoming vehicles?
- Is there a possibility of as yet unseen vehicles approaching at high speed?
- What is happening behind? Are any of the following vehicles likely to overtake me?
- What distance do I need to overtake and regain a nearside gap safely?
- What is an appropriate speed to complete the overtake, taking account of the hazards beyond the vehicle I'm overtaking?

Your priorities will change as you go through the manoeuvre. Continue to observe, plan and process information so that you can adjust your hazard priorities as the overtake develops. Observe what is happening in the far distance, the middle distance, the immediate foreground and behind; do this repeatedly. Remember that good observation alone is not enough: your safety depends on correctly interpreting what you see. See page 138 for examples of situations where drivers do not correctly interpret what they see.

In some cases, you might plan to take the following position but then find as you close up on the vehicle in front that you have a clear view of the road ahead and there are no additional hazards. In this case, you could go straight to the overtaking position.

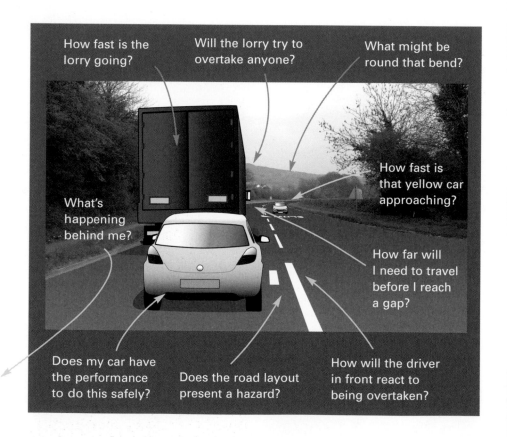

# Overtaking position

*The overtaking position is generally closer than the following position and minimises the distance you have to travel to overtake. It also shows the driver in front that you wish to overtake.*

*Position your vehicle to get the best possible view and opportunity to overtake, with due regard for safety.*

Plan to move into the overtaking position when you see a safe opportunity opening up (for example on the approach to a bend which opens into a straight stretch of road) so that you are ready to move out when it does.

Consider the need to signal. Adjust your speed to that of the vehicle in front. If you are not already in the most responsive gear for your speed, select the gear you will use to accelerate as you overtake.

Watch carefully for any new hazards. If a hazard comes into sight consider dropping back until you have passed it. Remember, if in doubt hold back.

How close you move to the vehicle in front depends on your assessment of visible hazards and possible dangers, and your need to maintain an adequate view of the road ahead. The exact position depends on good judgement and experience. The larger the vehicle in front, the further back you need to be. Also be aware that you might intimidate the driver in front if you are too close.

In the overtaking position, you may have less time to react to the actions of the vehicle in front, so you must be sure that there are no hazards ahead which might cause it to brake suddenly. You can only know this if you have been able to fully observe the road ahead.

With large vehicles and where it helps, take a view along both sides of the vehicle.

# Overtaking

From the overtaking position continue observing until you see an opportunity to overtake.

Position your vehicle so that you have a clear path beyond the vehicle you wish to pass, without accelerating.
From this position:

- if you see the manoeuvre would not be safe, return to the following or overtaking position as appropriate

- if the manoeuvre can be completed safely, accelerate past.

As you accelerate past, reconsider the hazards ahead of the overtaken vehicle. This may include other vehicles you want to overtake, or physical features such as junctions or bends.

## Overtaking more than one vehicle or in a line of traffic

If there is more than one vehicle, you may wish to consider a series of overtakes as one manoeuvre. While you may be able to plan these as one manoeuvre, each one should be reappraised separately as the vehicles are approached.

From the point of accelerating past the previous vehicle in the line you should consider whether to continue or to return to a safe position in the line yourself. Each of these decisions is a separate application of the system.

Don't be tempted to increase your speed for each overtake in a line of traffic.

Reappraise the opportunities for further overtakes and re-apply the system.

## Summary

The diagram below summarises the principles of overtaking one or more moving hazards.

Is there a safe opportunity to overtake?

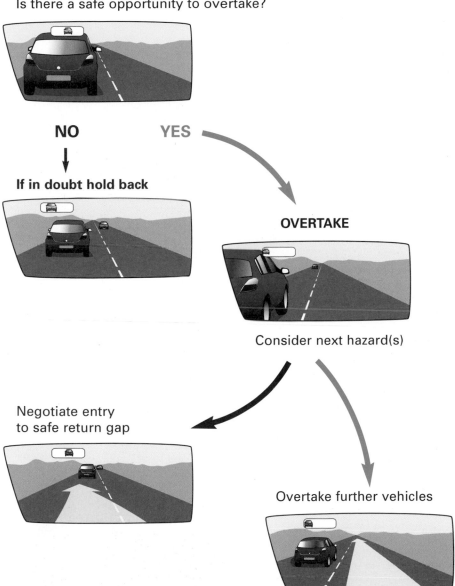

**NO**

**YES**

**If in doubt hold back**

**OVERTAKE**

Consider next hazard(s)

Negotiate entry to safe return gap

Overtake further vehicles

# Special hazards you must consider before overtaking

We have worked through two methods for overtaking systematically in straightforward conditions. But in practice, there are many hazards to overtaking in most everyday road and traffic situations. The illustrations below show some common overtaking collisions.

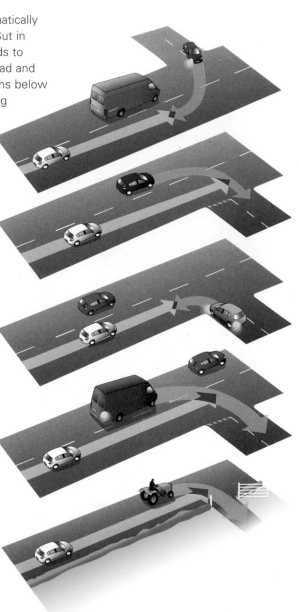

The driver of the white car does not realise that the driver of the blue car can only see the slow-moving van and may pull out onto the main road

The driver of the white car does not anticipate that the red car may turn without warning into the side road

The driver of the white car does not realise the driver of the green car is looking only to his right and may pull out

The driver of the white car thinks the van is indicating to overtake the car ahead, but the van is turning right

The driver of the white car does not anticipate that the tractor may turn without warning into an entrance or gateway

## The range of hazards you must consider

Before overtaking you must consider the full range of possible hazards that each situation presents:

- the vehicle in front
- the vehicles behind
- pedestrians
- oncoming vehicles not yet in view
- the road layout and conditions
- road surface
- overtaking in a stream of vehicles
- overtaking on a single carriageway
- right-hand bends
- left-hand bends
- overtaking on a dual carriageway.

You will also need to note any relevant road signs before attempting to overtake.

Some of these hazards are discussed in more depth below.

## The vehicle in front

Assess what sort of hazard the vehicle in front presents.

- Has the driver of the vehicle noticed you?
- Can you predict from earlier behaviour whether the driver's response is likely to be aggressive?
- Does the size or the load of the vehicle prevent the driver from seeing you or prevent you from seeing the road ahead clearly?
- Does the vehicle have left-hand drive (e.g. a foreign lorry)?

Signal your intention to overtake to the driver in front. Your road position and following distance help you to do this, but take care not to appear aggressive. This can be counterproductive and provoke an aggressive response in the other driver, who might speed up as you try to overtake. If the driver in front appears to be obstructive, consider whether it is worth overtaking at all. If you decide to go ahead, think about how much extra speed and space you need to allow.

If the driver in front has not noticed you, or has a load which obscures the rear view mirrors, consider using your headlights to signal that you are there.

Take extra care before overtaking a long vehicle or vehicles with wide or high loads. Assess the road ahead very carefully for any possible dangers. If you can, take views to both sides of the vehicle and make sure you have plenty of space to overtake and return safely to your own side.

## The vehicles behind

Assess whether the vehicles behind pose a risk. Note their speed, position and progress, and judge whether any of them may want to overtake you. Look out particularly for motorcycles. Be aware that other following vehicles could overtake the vehicle following you. Decide whether you need to signal. Use your mirrors to monitor the situation behind you, especially before changing your speed or position.

# Road layout and conditions

When you plan to overtake, look for possible hazards in the layout of the road ahead. Watch out for nearside obstructions or junctions — including pathways, tracks, entrances, and farm gates. Vehicles, pedestrians or animals could emerge from these causing the vehicle(s) in front of you to veer towards the centre of the road. Look for right-hand junctions and entrances concealing vehicles or other hazards that could move out into your path.

Look for lay-bys on both sides of the road and watch out for vehicles pulling out of them. Drivers pulling out of a lay-by on the other side of the road may not see you because they are watching what is happening behind rather than in front of them.

Assess the width of the road and look out for any features in the road which could obscure your view such as bends, hidden dips, hill crests and hump back bridges. There may be fast-moving vehicles approaching you on the sections of road you cannot see. Follow the basic rule for overtaking:

- Identify a gap into which you can return and the point along the road at which you will be able to enter it.

- Judge whether you will be able to reach that point before any oncoming vehicle, seen or unseen, could come into conflict with you.

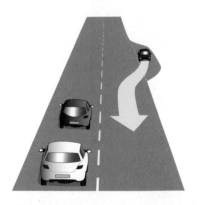

You should have observed the whole stretch of road necessary to complete the manoeuvre, and know that it does not include any other hazards. Look especially for hazards which might

Be wary of overtaking when approaching lay-bys as a vehicle could move out into your path.

cause the vehicles you are overtaking to alter their position. Make full use of road signs and road markings, especially those giving instructions or warning you of hazards ahead.

## The basic rule for overtaking

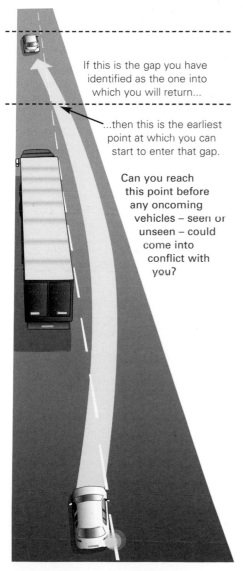

If this is the gap you have identified as the one into which you will return...

...then this is the earliest point at which you can start to enter that gap.

Can you reach this point before any oncoming vehicles – seen or unseen – could come into conflict with you?

## Road surface

Before you overtake, observe the condition of the road surface and note anything which could throw your vehicle off course or affect your visibility (e.g. loose gravel). Watch out for surface water which could cause a curtain of spray at a critical moment. Be aware that bad weather can affect how your vehicle holds the road and how well you can see the road.

See Chapter 2, *Observation and anticipation*, page 35.

## Overtaking in a stream of vehicles

Overtaking in a stream of vehicles is more difficult because it takes more time. You also have to take into account the possible actions of more drivers, both in front and behind. Drivers in front may not be aware that you are there or intend to overtake; drivers behind might try to overtake you. Always signal your intentions clearly to other road users.

Before you overtake, identify a clear gap between the vehicles in front which you can enter safely. Be aware that the gap may get smaller before you arrive, so choose gaps that are large enough to allow for this. Don't overtake if you will have to force your vehicle into a gap.

When planning to overtake in a stream of vehicles, consider moving out onto the other side of the road to give yourself a clearer view of the road ahead. Hold this position if you can see that the road ahead is clear, and if you can identify a clear return gap and have enough time to reach it. Allow for the possibility that the driver following you might move up into the gap that you have just left, preventing you from returning to it. When you reach the first return gap you may not need to enter it. If it is safe, hold your position while you decide whether you can overtake more vehicles.

When you plan to overtake clusters of vehicles, you must take extra care to ensure that the other drivers know you are there.

Where a queue has formed because of an obstruction in the road ahead, never try to jump the queue. It annoys other road users and can be dangerous.

When planning to overtake in a stream of vehicles, consider moving out onto the other side of the road to give yourself a clearer view of the road ahead.

## Overtaking on a single carriageway

This is perhaps the most hazardous form of overtaking because you put your vehicle in the path of any oncoming vehicles – so plan this manoeuvre with great care. Remember you can always reconsider your decision and hold back.

You need to be able to judge the speed and distance of oncoming vehicles accurately to assess whether you can reach the return gap before they do. Judging the speed of oncoming vehicles can be extremely difficult, especially on long straight roads. The size and type of the oncoming vehicle can give you clues about its possible speed.

As well as looking for vehicles, train yourself to look specifically for motorcyclists, cyclists and pedestrians before you overtake. Drivers often fail to spot the unexpected.

See Chapter 2, *Observation and anticipation*, page 25, Looking but not seeing.

## Overtaking on bends

In certain circumstances, it is possible to get a good clear view of the road on the other side of the bend before you enter it and, if you are sure there are no other hazards, to position yourself to overtake before the road straightens out. But overtaking on bends is potentially dangerous and you should always ensure that you have the available view to do this safely.

## Left-hand bends

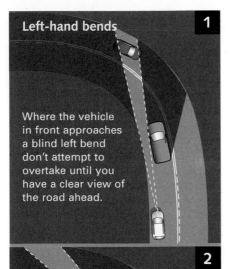

**1**

Where the vehicle in front approaches a blind left bend don't attempt to overtake until you have a clear view of the road ahead.

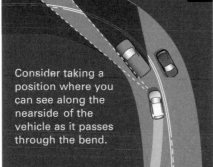

**2**

Consider taking a position where you can see along the nearside of the vehicle as it passes through the bend.

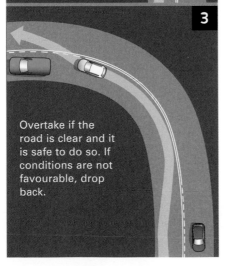

**3**

Overtake if the road is clear and it is safe to do so. If conditions are not favourable, drop back.

## Right-hand bends

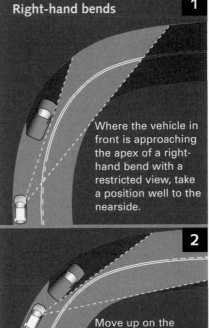

**1**

Where the vehicle in front is approaching the apex of a right-hand bend with a restricted view, take a position well to the nearside.

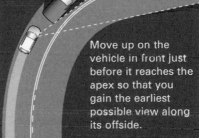

**2**

Move up on the vehicle in front just before it reaches the apex so that you gain the earliest possible view along its offside.

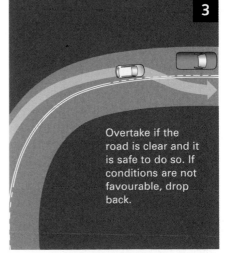

**3**

Overtake if the road is clear and it is safe to do so. If conditions are not favourable, drop back.

## Single carriageway roads marked with three lanes

Single carriageway roads marked with three lanes are potentially very dangerous as traffic in both directions shares the centre lane for overtaking. Never try to overtake if there is the possibility of an oncoming vehicle moving into the centre lane. Avoid overtaking when you would make a third line of moving vehicles unless you are sure it is absolutely safe to do so.

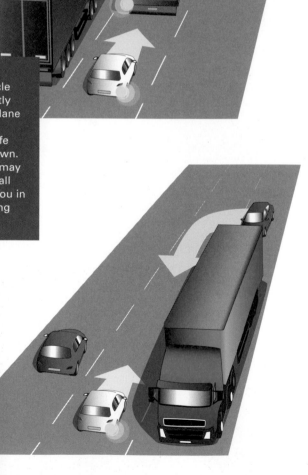

Don't be tempted to follow another vehicle through an apparently safe gap on a three-lane single carriageway. Always identify a safe return gap of your own. The vehicle in front may slip safely into a small return gap leaving you in the middle lane facing oncoming vehicles.

When you are planning to overtake, always look out for the 'lurker' who closes right up unseen behind other vehicles and then sweeps out to overtake. Never assume that the drivers of light vehicles behind an oncoming lorry will stay put. They could well pull out just when you do.

## Overtaking on multi-lane carriageways

On multi-lane carriageways it can be more difficult to judge the speed of traffic approaching from behind.

Before overtaking check the intentions of drivers in the nearside lanes. If a vehicle is closing up on the one in front, the driver may pull out without signalling or only signalling after the vehicle starts to move out. Watch the distance between the wheels of the vehicle and the lane markings. If the gap narrows, the vehicle could be moving out. Follow the key principles:

- to leave yourself room for manoeuvre at all times, generally avoid overtaking three abreast. (This may be unavoidable if traffic is dense.)

- only overtake on the nearside if traffic in all lanes is moving in queues.

- take particular care when planning to overtake large vehicles at roundabout exits and on left hand bends.

See Chapter 10, *Driving on motorways and other multi-lane carriageways.*

# Helping other drivers to overtake

Helping other drivers to overtake eases tensions and contributes to a cooperative driving culture that increases safety. Use your mirrors and be alert to the intentions of drivers behind you. If another driver wants to overtake you, make it easier by leaving enough distance between you and the vehicle in front to give them a safe return gap.

Be aware that other drivers may try to overtake you when you keep to the legal speed limit. This is quite likely when you slow down to enter or as you are about to leave a lower speed limit area.

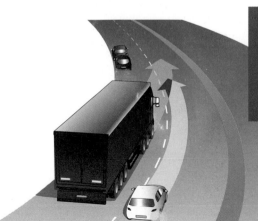

Where a large vehicle such as a lorry or coach is blocking your view of lane 1, hold your position until you can see that lane 1 is clear ahead. Then continue with the overtaking manoeuvre.

# Review

**In this chapter we have looked at:**

- how to overtake safely
- how to overtake where there are no other hazards
- the three-stage approach to overtaking when other hazards cause you to take up a following position
- the range of hazards to consider before overtaking.

## Check your understanding

Why is overtaking potentially hazardous?

What are the seven key safety points for overtaking?

Give an example of a hazard that would make you decide to follow another vehicle before overtaking.

What is the three-stage approach to overtaking and when is it used?

When you move out before overtaking, what should you check?

Why do you need to consider the driver in front before overtaking?

How might road layout and conditions affect overtaking?

When can it be useful to hold a position on the other side of the road?

How can you help others to overtake? Why is this important?

If you have difficulty in answering any of these questions, look back over the relevant part of this chapter to refresh your memory.

# Chapter 10
# Driving on motorways and multi-lane carriageways

**Use this chapter to find out about:**

- the special features of motorways
- how to join and leave the motorway
- how to drive safely on the motorway and other fast-moving multi-lane carriageways
- how to deal with specific hazards on motorways and multi-lane carriageways.

# Developing your skill at driving on multi-lane carriageways

Safe driving on motorways and other fast-moving multi-lane carriageways depends on rigorously applying the driving skills and methods explained in *Roadcraft* and developing your awareness of the extra hazards that arise on these roads.

Despite the high speed and volume of motorway traffic, motorways have the lowest accident rate of all UK roads. However, other fast-moving multi-lane roads such as dual carriageways combine traffic moving at equally high speed with additional hazards such as junctions to right and left, roundabouts, slow-moving vehicles and the absence of a hard shoulder (see page 161).

Much of the content of this chapter applies equally to all multi-lane carriageways, but motorways have some specific features which you will need to take into account:

- slip roads for entering and leaving the motorway (not always present on other multi-lane carriageways)
- limited opportunities for refreshment and refuelling
- the dangers of stopping on the hard shoulder in an emergency
- legal restrictions on which vehicles can use the motorway.

It takes time to develop accuracy in assessing speeds and stopping distances under fast-moving driving conditions. Always drive well within your own competence and aim to steadily develop your experience so that you are comfortable and confident within your existing speed range before moving on to higher speeds. Plan how you are going to address the fast-moving traffic conditions before you start your journey.

# Before you join a fast-moving road

## Prepare yourself

High speeds mean that hazardous situations develop quickly and that you travel further before you can react. At speed, minimum stopping distances are much longer and collisions often cause serious injury and damage. As the volume of traffic increases, the demands on your concentration and decision-making also increase. With more vehicles there are more hazards and less room to manoeuvre.

For all these reasons, you need to maintain a high level of concentration. This is more difficult in monotonous conditions such as driving for long periods in low density traffic, or in fog or at night. Prepare for your journey – assess your state of mind and plan how you will deal with feelings such as tiredness or low mood (for example, by driving more slowly or taking breaks). This is particularly important on motorways where there are limited opportunities to stop. Remember also to take account of the possible effects of any medication.

In difficult or demanding driving situations, be aware of the possible effects of stress. Police drivers are trained to respond to urgent calls without taking undue risks. But research shows that all drivers who feel their journey is urgent, either because of time pressure or because of the purpose of the journey, can experience increased stress which in turn can affect information processing, decision-making and judgement. A sense of urgency does not give the right to take risks. No emergency is so great that it justifies the possibility of injuring or killing someone through bad driving.

See Chapter 1, *Mental skills for better driving*, and Chapter 2, *Observation and anticipation*.

## Check your vehicle

Your vehicle needs to be in good condition and comply with legal and safety requirements so do a roadworthiness check before starting your journey. Stopping on the hard shoulder (if there is one) is dangerous for the occupants of the stationary vehicle and for other motorway users because there is a high risk of collision.

See Roadworthiness check, page 164.

## Plan your route

Plan your route and identify your point of exit and possible rest points before you travel, especially if you are using a motorway. Never consult a map while you are driving.

## Anticipate likely road conditions

Allow for the likely traffic volume and the possibility of roadworks or other delays so that you are not rushing your journey. If there are likely to be a lot of delays, consider another route or postpone your journey. Where weather conditions are deteriorating, consider carefully whether the journey is essential. Your safety depends on adapting your driving to the prevailing road and weather conditions and this is crucial on roads with fast-moving traffic.

Driving on motorways and multi-lane carriageways

# Joining the motorway

## Which lane is which?

Here we use the numbering system used by the police and other emergency services to refer to the lanes on motorways and other multi-lane carriageways.

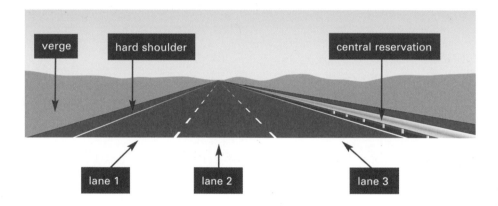

The nearside lane is lane 1, the next is lane 2 and so on. On a three-lane motorway lane 1 is the lane next to the hard shoulder and lane 3 is the lane next to the central reservation. The hard shoulder is not counted as a carriageway lane.

Joining the motorway at a slip road or where motorways merge is hazardous and you should use the system of car control to approach and join. Slip roads are designed to give drivers the time and space to merge smoothly with traffic on the main carriageway without causing other drivers to alter position or

speed. They are often raised, so take advantage of the high viewpoint to observe the traffic flow and to plan your approach. Drivers on the motorway have priority and may not be able to move over to allow you to enter lane 1, but looking early, planning and using your acceleration sense will enable you to merge safely. Only poor planning or exceptionally heavy traffic should cause you to stop in the slip road.

Slip roads have one or more lanes. If you are travelling in the outside lane of the slip road, consider how your speed and position will affect vehicles in the

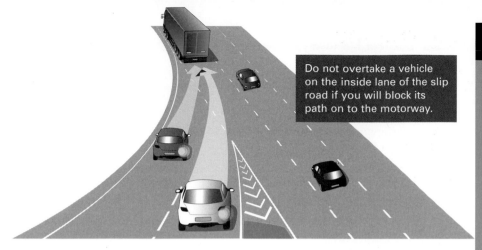

Do not overtake a vehicle on the inside lane of the slip road if you will block its path on to the motorway.

inside lane. If you overtake a vehicle on your nearside just before you join the motorway you could block its path. You risk colliding with it if you cannot move straight into lane 2 of the motorway.

# Use the system

As you enter the motorway, take in **information** about the traffic on the slip road and motorway so that you are in the correct **position**, at the correct **speed** and in the correct **gear** to **accelerate** onto the motorway smoothly and safely.

## Signalling

Well before you enter lane 1, decide whether you need to signal to let motorists on the motorway know that you intend to join the traffic flow.

Before you join the motorway, check over your shoulder to make sure there is nothing in your blind spot.

## Acceleration

Allow yourself time to adjust to the higher motorway speed and to gauge the speeds of other vehicles.

## Observation

Because of the speeds involved, it is vital to extend your observation:

- look ahead and behind you right up to the road horizons

- scan ahead, to the sides and to the rear frequently and thoroughly

- use your mirrors regularly – you should always know what is happening behind you

- be aware of your own and other drivers' blind spots and be prepared to move your body and alter vehicle position to observe what is happening in those areas

- monitor what is happening to your vehicle – regularly check that the instruments are giving normal readings and listen to the sound of

On your next motorway journey, practise extending your observation.

Make a point of scanning as far as the road horizon, front and back. Use your mirrors frequently. Regularly scan to the sides as well.

Aim to give yourself the longest possible time in which to react. Active scanning helps you to maintain a generally high level of attention, which increases your overall safety.

your engine and to the noise of the tyres on the road surface

- check your speed regularly – it is very easy to increase speed without realising.

When you are travelling in the outside lane of a fast-moving multi-lane carriageway, your last mirror check should be the nearside mirror as your area of greatest danger is from vehicles in lane 1 or lane 2.

## Adapting to higher speeds

At 70 mph you travel 31 metres (about three coach lengths) per second. To give yourself as much time to react as possible:

- extend your observations in all directions and to the road horizons

- anticipate early and maintain a safe following distance – in good weather the two-second rule is a good guide but in bad weather you must allow a much greater distance

- avoid coarse steering at speed

- give other drivers enough time to see your signals before making a manoeuvre

- use your headlights to alert other drivers to your presence.

## Lane discipline

You need good lane discipline for safe motorway driving. There are no slow or fast lanes. Overtake only to the right, except when traffic is moving in queues and the queue on your right is moving more slowly than you are.

*Do not move to a lane on your left to overtake.*

## Overtaking

Before you overtake watch out for:

- slower vehicles moving out in front of you

- faster vehicles coming up behind you.

Apply the system of car control to overtake safely on motorways and other multi-lane carriageways, paying special attention to taking, using and giving information.

## Taking information

Scan regularly so that you are continually aware of what the surrounding traffic is doing. You should know which vehicles are closing up on other vehicles in front, and which vehicles are moving up behind. Constantly monitor opportunities to overtake and match your speed of approach to coincide with an opportunity. Make allowances for the additional hazards presented by lane closures and motorway junctions.

Look for early warnings that other drivers intend to overtake:

- **relative speeds**
- **head movements**
- **body movements**
- **vehicle movement** from the centre of the lane towards the white lane markers.

You are likely to see all these before the driver signals: many drivers only signal as they start to change lanes.

Over a motorway journey of reasonable length (say 20 miles), **practise spotting these warning signs** to predict when other drivers are about to change lanes.

Use this anticipation to help your planning.

Think carefully before overtaking on left-hand bends where there are mainly heavy goods or large vehicles in lanes 1 and 2. A car may be hidden between the heavy goods vehicles and be about to pull out into lane 3. Make sure you can stop safely within the distance you can see to be clear. Do not attempt to overtake unless you are sure you can see **all** the vehicles in lane 2.

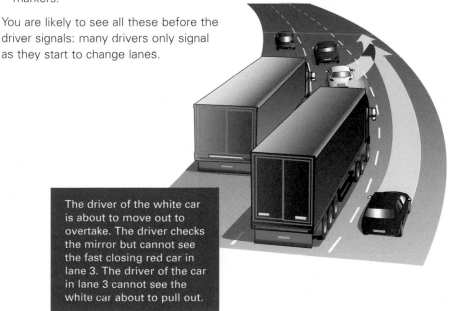

The driver of the white car is about to move out to overtake. The driver checks the mirror but cannot see the fast closing red car in lane 3. The driver of the car in lane 3 cannot see the white car about to pull out.

Driving on motorways and multi-lane carriageways

Just before you overtake, carefully check the position and speed of the vehicles behind. For example, before you move into lane 2 to overtake a vehicle in lane 1, check there are no fast closing vehicles moving back into lane 2 from lane 3.

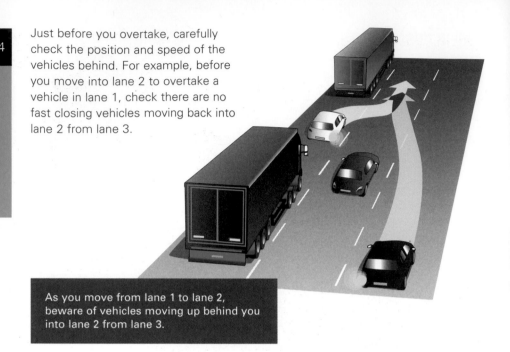

As you move from lane 1 to lane 2, beware of vehicles moving up behind you into lane 2 from lane 3.

Move your head to increase your view either side of your blind spot. Re-check the position and speed of vehicles to the front and then consider the information that you need to give to the surrounding traffic.

## Giving information

Avoid sitting in the blind spot of a vehicle you are trying to overtake. If you find that you are unable to overtake, drop back slightly so that you are visible to the driver.

Consider alerting other drivers to your presence especially if you are travelling at speed. If you decide a headlight flash would be helpful, give it in plenty of time for the other driver to react. Give a single flash: decide on the length of

flash according to your speed and the response of other drivers. Take care not to appear aggressive to other drivers, and avoid dazzling oncoming drivers. Be aware that flashing headlights could be misinterpreted by other drivers as an invitation to move out in front of you.

## Indicator signals

Consider indicating before changing lanes. Let the indicator flash long enough for other drivers to see and react to it.

When you have passed the vehicle or vehicles in front, return to the appropriate lane when you see an opportunity. Avoid constantly weaving in and out.

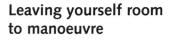

# Leaving yourself room to manoeuvre

In heavy traffic conditions be aware of the space around you and always try to avoid situations which leave you no room for manoeuvre if a hazard arises.

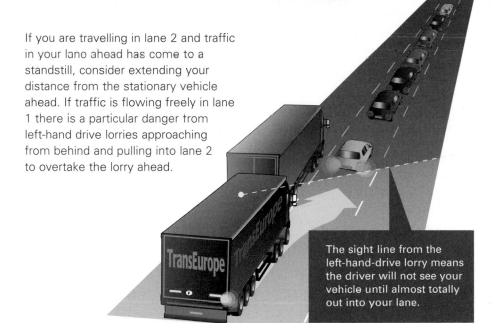

The driver of the white car has no room for manoeuvre if a hazard arises. Lanes 1 and 2 are blocked by lorries and lane 3 is blocked by the red car ahead. The white car could hold back until the red car has moved ahead of the lorries, but the driver must watch his mirror for vehicles closing up fast behind.

If you are travelling in lane 2 and traffic in your lane ahead has come to a standstill, consider extending your distance from the stationary vehicle ahead. If traffic is flowing freely in lane 1 there is a particular danger from left-hand drive lorries approaching from behind and pulling into lane 2 to overtake the lorry ahead.

The sight line from the left-hand-drive lorry means the driver will not see your vehicle until almost totally out into your lane.

TransEurope

### Being overtaken

Anticipate what the drivers behind you intend to do by their lane position and their speed of approach. This will help you to avoid potentially dangerous situations. As the other vehicle overtakes you, be aware that you are in the overtaking driver's blind spot.

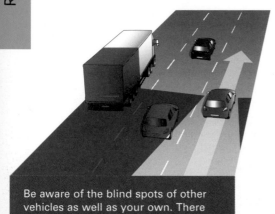

Be aware of the blind spots of other vehicles as well as your own. There are some positions in which you cannot be seen.

# Motorway junctions

At junctions and service areas, you are likely to meet variations in traffic speed and more vehicles changing lanes. Watch for drivers who only change lanes for an exit at the last minute. When you see a motorway exit, anticipate a slip road ahead and the possibility of traffic joining the motorway.

If you are on the main carriageway, check your mirrors early and allow traffic to join the motorway by making slight adjustments to your speed or changing lane. Vehicles on the motorway have right of way so don't do this if it would force other drivers to change their speed or position.

Watch for drivers changing lanes for an exit road at the last minute and watch for traffic joining the motorway at the slip road ahead.

# Leaving the motorway

Plan your exit. Make sure you know your exit junction well in advance. Assess the road and traffic conditions as you approach the junction and use the information provided by road signs and markings.

The diagram on the right shows a typical sequence of information given at motorway exits. Note that some newer motorways have signs at 1/3 mile and 2/3 mile so always read distance marker signs carefully.

As you approach your exit junction look for the advance direction signs and use the system of car control to plan and carry out your exit. If the motorway is busy, consider joining lane 1 earlier rather than later. If a signal is necessary, always allow plenty of time for other drivers to react. Indicate at the 300 yard marker.

There is usually a route direction sign at the point where the **exit road splits** from the main carriageway

**The North Sheffield Leeds**

**Nottingham A52**

25

A third directions sign at the **beginning of the exit road** adds principal destinations ahead

There are marker posts at **300, 200** and **100** yards before the start of the exit road

**Nottingham A52**

25 ½m

At **half a mile** from the exit a direction sign repeats the information

**Nottingham A52**

25 1m

**One mile** from the exit a direction sign gives the junction number and the roads leading off the exit with the town or destination names

Avoid braking on the main carriageway if possible and plan to lose any unwanted road speed in the exit road which provides a deceleration lane. On busy motorways watch out for vehicles leaving the motorway at the last minute from lanes 2 or 3 and cutting across your path.

Driving at high speed affects your perception of speed when you leave the motorway:

- check your speedometer regularly to help you adjust to the slower speeds of ordinary roads

- plan for the point at which you will meet two-way traffic

- be ready for acute bends at the end of motorway exit roads

- watch out for oil and tyre dust deposits which can make these areas exceptionally slippery.

**Assess how well you use the system of car control to leave a motorway.**

Practise starting a motorway exit from positions in lanes 1, 2 and 3. Pay particular attention to information processing.

- Did you exit the motorway smoothly and safely?

- Did you consider all the relevant phases of the system?

If not, consider how you could improve the manoeuvre next time.

# Bad weather conditions on fast-moving roads

Chapter 2 explained how weather conditions affect your ability to observe and anticipate. This section looks at planning for bad weather conditions at higher speeds.

See Chapter 2, *Observation and anticipation*, page 35, Weather conditions.

Bad weather reduces visibility and tyre grip so is more dangerous at high speed because you need a much greater overall safe stopping distance. You should always be able to stop safely in the distance you can see to be clear.

When you cannot see clearly, reduce your speed and consider using headlights and foglights. You must use them if visibility drops below 100 metres. The gap between motorway marker posts is about 100 metres so use these to assess how far you can see. Bear in mind that foglights can mask your brakelights and dazzle the driver behind so switch them off as soon as visibility improves.

## Fog

Fog reduces your perception of speed and risk because you can't see; at the same time it encourages you to drive close enough to keep in sight the vehicle lights ahead. Watch out for reckless behaviour of other drivers.

In freezing fog, mist and spray can freeze on to the windscreen at higher

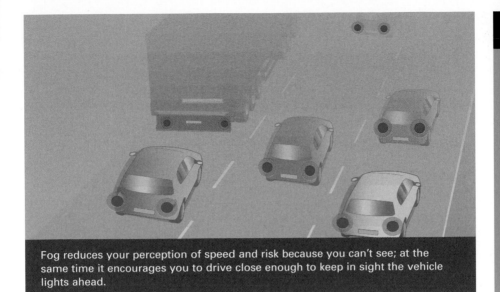

Fog reduces your perception of speed and risk because you can't see; at the same time it encourages you to drive close enough to keep in sight the vehicle lights ahead.

speeds, reducing visibility further. To stop within the distance you can see to be clear in variable fog, adjust your speed to the actual density of the fog banks you are driving through, not to some imagined 'safe' speed for foggy conditions. Driving in fog is very tiring. If you start to feel tired, stop and take regular rests.

## Rain

High speeds increase the hazards from rain and water lying on the road surface. Heavy spray from tyres cutting through water can reduce visibility to a few feet, especially as you overtake large vehicles. Water lying on the road surface can build up to form a wedge of water between the tyres and the road, causing aquaplaning with instant and complete loss of control.

See Chapter 5, *Maintaining vehicle stability*, page 97, Aquaplaning, for further advice.

After a long, hot, dry spell a deposit of tyre and other dust builds up on the road surface. These deposits create a slippery surface especially during and after rain. Avoid heavy breaking, steering or accelerating or you could lose tyre grip.

## Snow, sleet and ice

Snow and sleet reduce visibility and tyre grip. At speed, spray thrown up by the wheels of the vehicle in front reduces visibility further, and when ruts develop in the snow it may be difficult to steer. In heavy snow consider whether your journey is really necessary.

Reduce speed and increase following distances in icy conditions, especially if the road surface is not gritted.

## High winds

Sections of carriageway that are raised above the surrounding countryside are affected by high winds. Be prepared for particularly strong gusts of wind as you leave a cutting, enter or emerge from under a bridge, cross a dale or go into open country. Take particular care on viaducts and bridges.

## Bright sun

Bright sun low in the sky can cause serious dazzle, especially on east/west sections of road: use your visors to reduce dazzle. If the sun is shining in your mirrors, adjust them to give you the best visibility with minimum glare. If you are dazzled by bright sun, other drivers may be too so allow for this when overtaking.

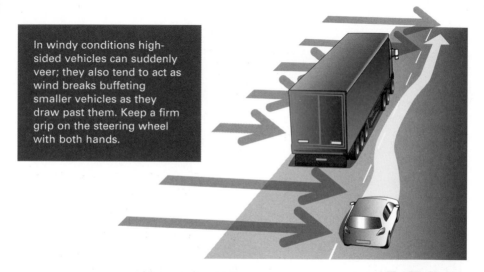

In windy conditions high-sided vehicles can suddenly veer; they also tend to act as wind breaks buffeting smaller vehicles as they draw past them. Keep a firm grip on the steering wheel with both hands.

High-sided vehicles create a slip stream which tends to pull smaller vehicles towards them during overtaking. As the smaller vehicle moves in front it breaks free of the suction and tends to veer out. Correct this with a firm grip and appropriate pressure on the steering wheel.

# Other hazards

## Debris

Regularly scan the road surface for debris which may have fallen from vehicles. This can damage tyres and cause other vehicles to suddenly alter position.

## Lane closures

Roadworks are a regular feature of motorway journeys. Contraflow systems are not dangerous in themselves but become dangerous when drivers ignore advance warnings. All roadworks are signed on approach and you should know the sequence of signs. Keep to the mandatory speed limits through roadworks, even when conditions seem to be suitable for a higher speed.

Merging with other traffic requires judgement and courtesy. It is sensible for vehicles from each lane to merge alternately. But these situations often create conflict and result in collisions. Allow a reasonable following gap and never close up to prevent other vehicles merging.

Matrix signs and signals warn of lane closures or other changes in driving conditions ahead. You may not immediately be able to see the need to slow down or change lanes but don't assume the sign is a mistake. The incident may be some distance further along the motorway.

# Additional hazards on fast-moving multi-lane carriageways

On multi-lane carriageways you need to watch out for a range of additional hazards that are not present on motorways:

- slow-moving traffic
- traffic lights
- roundabouts
- right-hand junctions
- crossroads
- traffic moving into the right-hand lane to turn right
- traffic entering the carriageway from the central reservation
- traffic crossing the carriageway
- pedestrians crossing the carriageway
- entrances and exits other than road junctions (to services, petrol stations, restaurants, pubs)
- left-hand junctions with only a short (or no) slip road
- public footpath crossing the carriageway – indicated by an overlap in the central reservation safety barrier.

Driving on motorways and multi-lane carriageways

# Review

**In this chapter we have looked at:**

- the special features of motorways that make them hazardous
- safety points to consider before using motorways and fast-moving multi-lane carriageway
- how to join and leave the motorway
- the correct use of lanes on multi-lane carriageways
- the importance of extended observation, especially when driving at speed
- how to overtake on multi-lane carriageways
- the additional hazards presented by motorway junctions
- the effect of weather conditions and other special hazards

## Check your understanding

What are the special features of motorways?

List four things you should do to prepare for the journey before you join a multi-lane carriageway.

Why can it be hazardous to overtake a vehicle on the slip road just as you join a motorway?

Apart from indicator lights, what are the possible early signs that another vehicle is going to change lanes?

How are motorway exit junctions signed?

List three examples of weather conditions that are more hazardous at high speed and explain how you would deal with them.

Describe at least five hazards present on multi-lane carriageways that are not found on motorways.

If you have difficulty in answering any of these questions, look back over the relevant part of this chapter to refresh your memory.

# Appendices

**Know your vehicle**
- Roadworthiness check
- Pre-driving check
- Testing your brakes

**European Goals for Driver Education (GDE)**

**Key safety points**

**Glossary**

**Index**

# Know your vehicle

## Roadworthiness check

Before you start to drive you should ensure that your vehicle is roadworthy. Carry out the following checks:

- [ ] visual examination of the exterior for damage or defects
- [ ] tools and jack are present and in good order
- [ ] wheels in good order and nuts secure (do not over-tighten, especially with alloy wheels)
- [ ] tyres – check all the tyres, including the spare, for:
    - damage
    - tread depth
    - pressure (pressure settings are only accurate when tyres are cold)
    - compatibility of type
- [ ] adequate fuel, oil, water, windscreen wash and other fluids
- [ ] fan belt in good condition and correctly tensioned
- [ ] lights – including high intensity foglights, indicators, reversing and brakelights – in working order
- [ ] windscreen wipers and washers in good condition
- [ ] horn working correctly
- [ ] fire extinguisher present and in working order
- [ ] all glass clean – windows inside and out, lenses, mirrors.

A useful aid to remember the key points to check is:

# P  O  W  D  E  R

**P**etrol  **O**il  **W**ater  **D**amage  **E**lectrics  **R**ubber (tyres and wipers)

Carry out this check every time you get into a vehicle.

Make sure you are familiar with the position and operation of the controls, auxiliary controls and instruments before setting off:

- ☐ handbrake on, gear in neutral
- ☐ identify engine type; type of drive (front, rear or four wheel); type of gearbox (automatic or manual)
- ☐ identify active safety features (ABS, electronic stability control (ECS), traction control, adaptive suspension)
- ☐ adjust seat (position, rake and height if adjustable) to give good all round vision and good access to the controls; adjust head restraint so top is at least level with top of ears (to protect from whiplash)
- ☐ handbrake and footbrake respond firmly
- ☐ number and position of gears, position of reverse gear
- ☐ position of controls and auxiliaries
- ☐ doors are securely closed.

Switch on ignition, note warning lights; start engine.
Continue with these checks:

- ☐ after system becomes operational check the instruments; if any of the earlier checks could not be completed before ignition or start up, do them now
- ☐ carry out stationary brake test (see page 166) to ensure the system is working
- ☐ adjust mirrors, inside and out, to give best view
- ☐ make sure all the auxiliaries are working
- ☐ check gauges and warning lights
- ☐ check seat belt – not frayed or twisted, locks when tugged, releases on depressing the button, properly adjusted – and then fit it
- ☐ check in mirrors, select gear, do shoulder check, release handbrake (in automatics keep footbrake depressed before engaging DRIVE), move off when safe.

As soon as possible after moving off carry out a moving brake test (see over page). Check the gauges and warning lights at intervals during the journey, taking action if necessary.

# Testing your brakes

Check the brakes every time you use your vehicle, both before you move off and when the vehicle is moving.

## The stationary test

Check that the brake pedal moves freely and gives a firm positive pressure. Physically check that the handbrake secures the vehicle.

## The moving test

The purpose of the moving brake test is to:

• check that the vehicle pulls up in a straight line under progressive braking

• learn how much to press the brake pedal in that particular vehicle

• identify any unexpected problems.

Brakes are the most important part of the vehicle and a moving brake test is vital when you move off in an unfamiliar vehicle that you may need to drive in demanding conditions at higher speeds.

Test the footbrake as soon as possible after moving off. Always consider the safety and convenience of other road users before you do a moving test:

• Check the road is clear behind you, and accelerate briskly to reach 25-30mph.

• Declutch (to avoid engine braking interfering with the test).

• Gripping the wheel lightly, brake gradually and progressively, not harshly.

• Feel for anything unusual (e.g. a tendency to pull to one side, any vibration or pulsing through the brake pedal) and listen for anything unusual (e.g. noise from the brakes could mean they are binding).

• Release the pedal before you reach a standstill to check that the brakes release fully and are not binding.

# European Goals for Driver Education (GDE)

The GDE matrix is a European framework that sets out what driver training should focus on to produce the safest possible new drivers.

| The four levels that are involved in all driving tasks | Knowledge and skills you have to master | Risk-increasing factors that you need to be aware of | Evaluating yourself |
|---|---|---|---|
| **4.** Your goals for life and your skills for living | What are your life goals and values? How do you behave on your own and in a group? What's your 'style' and how does it affect your driving? | Be aware if you are under peer pressure to perform in a certain way. Do you have any habits or lifestyle dependencies that create an added driving risk? | Think about yourself. Are you impulsive and, if so, can you control your impulses? What are your motives for your actions? Examine your lifestyle and your values. |
| **3.** Your specific trip, its context and goals | Each trip is different, with different motives, goals and its own unique set of circumstances. This is about being aware of each trip and its particular context. | What is this particular journey for? Is it urgent? Are you under pressure? What are the driving conditions likely to be? | Ask yourself if you have planned adequately for this trip. Examine your personal feelings and expectations for the journey and why you undertook it. |
| **2.** Mastering each specific traffic situation | This is about observing, signalling, reading the road, assessing safety margins, obeying the rules, anticipating danger and positioning your vehicle to make safe progress. | This is about being aware of the specific driving conditions Are there vulnerable road-users? Is your speed in conflict with normal safety margins? Are you allowing for weather conditions? | How were your observation skills? Did you anticipate hazards and handle them safely? Assess your strengths and weaknesses for the trip. |
| **1.** Mastering each specific vehicle manoeuvre | This is about the physics of driving – knowing vehicles and how to handle them, particularly how they behave when braking, cornering and accelerating. | This is about the specific qualities of the vehicle you are driving. What technology is it fitted with? Does it handle in an idiosyncratic way? | Did you handle your vehicle well? Did the vehicle spring any surprises on you? Were you in perfect control throughout? Assess your strengths and weaknesses for the trip. |

# Key safety points

- Always drive so that you can stop safely within the distance you can see to be clear, by day or by night.

- Do not drive at speed unless you are competent, and it is safe to do so.

- Be familiar with the controls and the handling characteristics of your vehicle – use the controls smoothly.

- High-speed driving requires maximum attention – if you can't achieve a high level of concentration because of tiredness or some other cause, do not drive fast.

- If you double your speed, you quadruple your braking distance.

- Put into practice the skills developed in *Roadcraft* which are designed to increase your safety.

- Be aware of the onset of tiredness, and take a break.

- No emergency is so great that it justifies a collision – it is far better to arrive late than not at all.

# Glossary

## ABS

*See Antilock braking system*

## Acceleration sense

The ability to vary vehicle speed in response to changing road and traffic conditions by accurate use of the accelerator. *See page 64*

## Antilock braking system

A braking system which retains the ability to steer during harsh or emergency braking. Also known as ABS. *See page 89*

## Aquaplaning

A serious loss of steering and braking control caused by a wedge of water building up between the front tyres and the road surface. *See page 97*

## Auxiliaries

The auxiliary controls on a vehicle as distinct from the major controls. Examples of the auxiliaries are: horn, indicators, lights, wipers, washers, heater and ventilation controls. *See Controls, Instruments*

## Blind spots

Areas around a vehicle which the driver cannot see because the bodywork blocks sight or the mirrors do not cover these areas. *See page 155*

## Cadence or rhythm braking

In vehicles without ABS, a method of braking in slippery conditions which uses repeated application of the brakes to obtain some steering control while braking. The brakes are sharply applied to momentarily hold the wheels locked, and then released again to regain steering. This sequence is repeated deliberately until sufficient road speed is lost. Braking occurs while the brakes are on, steering while they are off. *See page 96*

## Camber

The convex slope across a road surface designed to assist drainage. Camber falls from the crown of the road to the edges. It has an effect on cornering which differs according to whether the bend is to the right or the left. *See page 121*

## Central differential

The differential in a four wheel drive vehicle which allows the front and rear wheels to revolve at different speeds.

## Controls

The major controls of a vehicle are the accelerator, brakes, clutch, gear-stick, steering wheel. *See Auxiliaries, Instruments*

## Cornering

Driving a car round a corner, curve or bend. Its meaning is not restricted to corners. Cornering is discussed in detail in Chapter 8.

### Cylinder compression

*See Engine compression*

### Electronic stability control (ESC)

An extension of antilock braking and traction control systems, ESC cuts in if a driver steers too sharply and may help prevent the resulting oversteer or understeer from developing into a skid. Also called electronic stability programme (ESP). *See page 90*

### Electronic stability programme (ESP)

*See previous entry*

### Engine compression

The compression of gases in the cylinders of an internal combustion engine. Compression uses energy so, when deceleration reduces the fuel supply to the engine, energy for compression is taken from the road wheels, thereby slowing them down.

### Following position

The distance at which it is safe to follow a vehicle in front. This distance varies according to the circumstances. *See page 133*

### Gears

The mechanism which converts the engine output into different speed and power combinations at the road wheels. A high gear drives the road wheels faster; a low gear drives the road wheels more slowly. In most cars the top gear is gear 4, 5 or 6; bottom gear is gear 1. Gears are discussed in Chapter 4.

### Hazard/hazardous

Anything that is an actual or potential danger. *See page 20*

### Information processing

The taking, using and giving of information is the central process on which all phases of the system of car control depend. *See page 50*

### Instruments

The gauges, dials, warning lights, etc. of a vehicle that give information about how it is functioning: for example, the speedometer, oil warning light and main beam indicator. *See Auxiliaries, Controls*

### Limit point

The furthest point to which you have an uninterrupted view of the road surface. On a level stretch of road this will be where the right-hand side of the road appears to meet the left-hand side of the road. The limit point is used in a system of cornering called limit point analysis. *See page 122*

### Nearside

The left side of a vehicle looking forward from the driver's position. *See Offside*

### Offside

The right side of a vehicle looking forward from the driver's position. *See Nearside*

## Oversteer

The tendency of a vehicle to turn more than you would expect for the amount of turn given to the steering wheel. Contrast with understeer. *See page 120*

## Overtaking position

The position adopted behind another vehicle in readiness to overtake when a safe opportunity arises. It is generally closer than the following position and may reduce the time you have to react to actions of the vehicle in front. It should only be adopted if you know there are no hazards ahead which might cause the vehicle in front to brake suddenly. *See page 135*

## POWDER check

An aid for remembering the key items to check before starting a journey: Petrol Oil Water Damage Electrics Rubber (tyres and wipers).
*See page 164*

## Pull–push steering

A steering technique. *See page 79*

## Reaction time

The time between gathering new information about a hazard and responding to it. Reaction time consists of decision time + response time.
*See page 6*

## Red mist

A mental and physiological state which drivers experience when they are so determined to achieve some non-driving objective, such as pursuing a vehicle in front, that they are no longer capable of assessing driving risks realistically. It is associated with a greatly increased accident risk.
*See page 12*

## Revs

The number of engine revolutions per minute.

## Rhythm braking

*See Cadence braking*

## Road users

Any user of the highway: vehicles, cyclists, pedestrians, runners, animals. The term is used to emphasise the need to be aware of everything on the highway, not just vehicles.

## Roadside marker posts

Posts marking the edge of the road, displaying red reflective studs on the nearside of the road and white reflective studs on the offside of the road.

## Rotational steering

A steering technique. *See page 80*

## Safe stopping distance rule

The basic safety rule for drivers: always drive so that you are able to stop safely within the distance you can see to be clear. This gives you a safe speed by relating your speed to your ability to stop. *See page 73*

### Scanning

A method of observation. The use of regular visual sweeps of the whole of the driving environment – the distance, the mid-ground, the foreground, sides and rear – to ensure that the driver is aware of everything that is happening. *See page 24*

### Superelevation

Superelevation is the banking up of a section of road towards the outside edge of the curve. This makes the slope favourable for cornering in both directions. *See page 121*

### The system – the system of car control

A methodical way of approaching and negotiating hazards that increases your safety by giving you more time to react to hazards. It involves careful observation, early anticipation and planning and a systematic use of the controls to maintain your vehicle's stability in all situations. The system is central to *Roadcraft*. It is fully explained in Chapter 3.

### Torque

The wheel turning power developed by an engine.

### Traction

The grip of a tyre on the road surface.

### Traction control systems

Traction control improves vehicle stability and assists steering by controlling excess wheel slip on individual wheels and reducing engine power to maintain tyre grip. *See page 90*

### Tyre grip trade-off

The tyre grip available in any given situation is limited, and is shared between accelerating, braking and steering forces. If more of the tyre grip is used for braking or accelerating, less will be available for steering. *See page 60*

### Understeer

The tendency of a vehicle to turn less than you expect for the amount of turn you give to the steering wheel. Contrast with oversteer. *See page 120*

# Index

Roadcraft

Index